HEBREW POEMS FROM SPAIN

THE LITTMAN LIBRARY OF
JEWISH CIVILIZATION

Dedicated to the memory of
LOUIS THOMAS SIDNEY LITTMAN
who founded the Littman Library for the love of God
and as an act of charity in memory of his father
JOSEPH AARON LITTMAN
and to the memory of
ROBERT JOSEPH LITTMAN
who continued what his father Louis had begun
יהא זכרם ברוך

'*Get wisdom, get understanding:*
Forsake her not and she shall preserve thee'
PROV. 4: 5

The Littman Library of Jewish Civilization is a registered UK charity
Registered charity no. 1000784

Hebrew Poems from Spain

◆

Introduction, Translation, and Notes by

DAVID GOLDSTEIN

London

The Littman Library of Jewish Civilization
in association with Liverpool University Press

The Littman Library of Jewish Civilization
Registered office: 4th floor, 7–10 Chandos Street, London W1G 9DQ

in association with Liverpool University Press
4 Cambridge Street, Liverpool L69 7ZU, UK
www.liverpooluniversitypress.co.uk/littman

Managing Editor: Connie Webber

Distributed in North America by
Oxford University Press Inc., 198 Madison Avenue,
New York, NY 10016, USA

First published 1965 by Routledge & Kegan Paul Ltd for
The Littman Library of Jewish Civilization
First issued in paperback 2007

Catalogue records for this book are available from the
British Library and the Library of Congress

ISBN 978–1–904113–66–9

Printed and bound in Great Britain by
CPI Group (UK) Ltd., Croydon, CR0 4YY

Foreword

RAYMOND SCHEINDLIN

I

When David Goldstein's little anthology appeared in 1965 it was a pioneering work, being the first anthology in English completely devoted to the poetry of the Hebrew Golden Age. At the time, the only translations of Golden Age poets widely available were the three volumes devoted to individual poets—Solomon Ibn Gabirol, Moses Ibn Ezra, and Judah Halevi—published by the Jewish Publication Society in the 1920s and 1930s. While these works were useful in their way, their scope was too narrow to convey the sweep of the literary activity of the Golden Age poets, and their stilted translations obscured the poems' literary value.

David Goldstein's anthology includes not only the best-known poets but some less familiar names, and ranges through the whole period, from the beginning of the Hebrew Golden Age, in the tenth century, to the end of the thirteenth. The inclusion of such less-known poets as Ibn Avitur, Ibn Khalfun, al-Harizi, and Ibn Zabara is a valuable demonstration that fame and quality are not correlative. The preservation of Hebrew poetry from the Middle Ages depended partly on chance, and many poets who are today obscure were deservedly considered leading literary figures in their time.

In adopting an unpretentious style of translation and relieving the poems of the rigid English verse patterns and biblical diction of the JPS volumes, Goldstein also did the poets a great favour. The biblical Hebrew of Golden Age Hebrew poetry may sound rather lofty to our ears, but the poets chose their style in part because they regarded biblical Hebrew as lucid and familiar; they wanted their poetry to be free of the kind of affectation that they saw in the synagogue poetry of their predecessors. True, they embellished their biblical Hebrew by making heavy use of the rhetorical devices typical of contemporary Arabic poetry; but Goldstein saw that the attempt to systematically reproduce these figures of speech, often so graceful in Hebrew, can result in an unbecoming artificiality in English. Goldstein was not a professional poet, but he based his translations on the fundamentally poetic insights that they should be simple and that the poets should be allowed to speak for themselves. We translators of medieval Hebrew poetry who have attempted to capture Golden Age style in English or to impose on the poets our own ideas about poetry have often come to regret our attempts to poetize poets who were much better at their craft than we.

Goldstein's work was followed in 1981 by a comprehensive anthology of Hebrew poetry from antiquity to the present, Ted Carmi's *The Penguin Book of Hebrew Verse*. This work contains an impressive selection of medieval poetry, including poems by major and minor figures of the Golden Age. It serves well as a textbook; but its double-columned pages crowded with dense prose translations and Hebrew text can be forbidding to the reader who is not already committed to the material. The pages of Goldstein's anthology, by contrast, are designed to display the poetry as poetry, with each line being given the breathing room appropriate for writing that was meant to be read slowly and pleasurably.

Thus Goldstein's anthology remains the easiest and most attractive introduction to the Hebrew Golden Age for the uninitiated. To such readers, it offers an informative introduction to the subject and a broad selection of the poets and their themes, with each poet being introduced by a thumbnail sketch of his life and career, and each poem accompanied by the barest explanatory notes that would be needed by the general reader.

II

David Goldstein may have been the better suited to create an anthology for the general reader in that he was not an academic specialist in medieval Hebrew literature but a scholarly rabbi with a superb knowledge of Hebrew, a love of poetry, and an aptitude for learned popularization. Born in London in 1933, he showed early aptitude in French, Latin, and Greek. He studied English literature at St Edmund Hall, Oxford, where he also wrote poetry and belonged to a literary circle. He received his MA in 1956, expecting to become an English teacher, but under the influence of the distinguished Talmud scholar Abraham Spiro he took up Jewish studies, receiving his doctorate from University College, London, and rabbinic ordination from Leo Baeck College. After serving as rabbi to two congregations, he joined the staff of the British Library's Department of Hebrew Manuscripts and Printed Books in 1975, eventually becoming Deputy Keeper in the Oriental Collection. He published *Hebrew Poems from Spain* while still serving as a pulpit rabbi; the book first appeared in England in 1965 and in the United States in 1966; a revised and expanded edition entitled *The Jewish Poets of Spain, 900–1250* was published by Penguin Books in 1971. Also in the spirit of learned popularization, he wrote a charming anthology of Jewish legends based on the Bible, entitled *Jewish Folklore and Legend* (1980).

But Goldstein also published works of a more technical nature. His introduction to *The Book of Proverbs with the Commentary of Immanuel of Rome* appeared in 1981, followed by three books that appeared in 1985: *The Ashkenazic Haggadah: A Hebrew Manuscript of the Mid-Fifteenth Century from the Collections of the British Library*, which won the silver medal at the Leipzig book fair; a bibliography, *Hebrew Incunables in the British Isles: A Preliminary Survey*; and *Hebrew Manuscript Painting*. He also edited a volume of essays by Joseph Weiss entitled *Studies in East European Jewish Mysticism and Hasidism*, which appeared in the same banner year. His most ambitious work was his translation of Isaiah Tishby's monumental *The Wisdom of the Zohar*, which received the Webber Prize in translation of the Oxford Centre for Postgraduate Hebrew Studies and which has become a major point of entry to the study of the recondite classic work of the kabbalah. On his early death in 1987, he was eulogized as the outstanding Hebrew scholar of Britain's Progressive Jewish community of his time.

Hebrew Poems from Spain remains the only anthology in English devoted entirely to the Golden Age with selections from all the major and some minor poets presented in verse translation. The book is a gift both to the academic world and to all readers interested in the literary achievements of the Jews. That it is being kept alive through this reissue is a source of joy to all who care about Jewish letters.

Contents

'The Sources of My Being' by Moses ibn Ezra first appeared in *The Jewish Quarterly*.

'Let Man Remember' and 'Where are the Graves?' by Moses ibn Ezra, and Halevi's 'Curtains of Solomon' first appeared in *The Liberal Jewish Monthly*.

I am grateful to the respective editors for their permission to reprint these poems here.

Introduction

TO SAY THAT THE POETRY OF THE JEWS has its beginning in the
literature of the Bible is true in more than one sense. It is true chrono-
logically; it is also true from the point of view of artistic and spiritual
inspiration. To the Jew of the Middle Ages the Bible represented the
revelation of the one God. It formed the basis for his whole religious
life, both through the reverence accorded to it as it was read and studied
in the synagogues, and through the legal, homiletical, and philosophical
writings of the Rabbis who searched endlessly for the divine truth
within its pages. There is little evidence that even the most cultured
Jews formed any aesthetic or literary critique of the Biblical writings.
The Bible was at one and the same time philosophy, law, history and
moral exhortation. But it was not 'literature'. *The Bible Designed to be
Read as Literature* is a comparatively modern phenomenon.

But, despite the lack of a literary theory of the Bible, there can be no
doubt that, in practice, the poetic books of the Bible made a deep im-
pression, as poetry, upon the Jewish consciousness; so much so, that one
can almost regard the products of the Spanish Hebrew poets as exten-
sions of the Hebrew poetry of an earlier time.

It is generally accepted that much of the older strata of the Biblical
literature is poetic in form. And this fits in with the theory that human
beings expressed themselves rhythmically and colourfully in poetry
first, and then proceeded to the logical lucidity of prose. At all events,
the song of the Hebrews at the crossing of the Red Sea (Exodus 15), and
the song of Deborah (Judges 5) are probably the earliest surviving
Hebrew literary records, and, more certainly, the earliest manifestations
of the Hebrew poetic genius—a genius which was to produce the
Psalms, Job, the Song of Songs, and the magnificent declamations of
the prophets.

Of all this poetry, only the Song of Songs is of an obviously secular
nature. Indeed, it was only because this poem was given a strictly

religious interpretation by the Rabbis, as we shall see later, that it was included in the canon at all. It is tempting to conjecture how much love-poetry of this kind was written by the Hebrews, and is now lost to us forever, because it was not regarded as Holy Writ. Certainly, we should never lose sight of the fact that the whole Biblical canon is but a selection of Hebrew literature, and we may well wonder what type of writing it was that was discarded.

After the close of the canon, we have to wait for more than a thousand years before Hebrew secular poetry appears again on the scene, as an important part of the renaissance of Hebrew poetry in Spain in the tenth century. What is the reason for this lack? We know that the Rabbis of the first centuries of the Christian era were familiar with Greek language and culture. Many Greek and Latin words found their way at this time into Hebrew. But officially imitation of non-Jewish models was frowned upon, and perhaps the lack of secular poetry is a result of this reluctance to embark upon an activity which might be construed to be contrary to the law and customs of the Jews. Philosophically speaking, too, even in the eyes of the Greeks themselves, the poet held a very low place in the ranks of the ideal society. There is always the possibility, however, that such poetry was written by Jews, but, because of its very nature, did not achieve that status which would have accorded it permanence.

For the poetry of the Jews, therefore, in the early centuries of the Christian era, we must turn to the Jews' religious writings, and especially to the domain of prayer. We might well say that some of the liturgical writing of the Tannaitic and Amoraic periods (100 B.C.E. to 600 C.E.) has an added poetic value for the very reason that it was not written primarily with poetic intent. This is poetry formed by the simple power of intense devotional fervour, not by the 'making' of the poet. It is surely right for Brody and Wiener's anthology of post-biblical Hebrew poetry to begin with prayers of this kind. Here is the first part of a prayer attributed to Rabbi Jochanan (first century):

> Lord of all worlds,
> Not because of our good deeds do we lay
>   our prayer before you,
> But because of your great mercies.
> What are we?
> What is our life?
> What is our love?
> What is our goodness?

2

What is our help?
What is our strength?
What is our power?
What shall we say before you
O Lord, our God, and God of our fathers?

All the mighty are as nothing before you,
And the men of renown as though they had not been,
And wise men are without knowledge,
And philosophers without discernment,
For all their acts are nothing,
And the days of their lives empty before you,
As it is written in your holy words:
'Man is not superior to the beast for all is vanity.'
(The complete prayer may be read in
Singer's Prayer Book, 1962, page 9.)

The Jews embellished their liturgy by writing *piyyutim*. The most well-known *piyyutim* are those of Eleazar Kalir (seventh century). The typical *piyyut* (the word is of Greek origin) suffers from its contrived construction, its unlimited verbal coinage, and its abstruse reference to Rabbinic exposition and elaboration of the Bible. It makes too great a demand on the intellectual agility of the reader (or listener) and the effort expended is often not justified by the result. However, the form of the *piyyut* continued to have an influence into and beyond the Spanish period. An example of its influence can be seen in the poem 'A Song for the New Year' by Joseph ibn Abithur, and many *piyyutim* still form part of traditional Jewish prayer-books. Its effect on Ashkenazi (Franco-German) communities was particularly strong.

The revival of Hebrew poetry was a direct consequence of two factors: the residence of the Jews in Muslim lands, and the Jews' reappraisal of the Bible.

The swift conquest by the Muslims of the coasts of the Southern Mediterranean, and their penetration into Spain affected every aspect of the lives of the Jews who came into contact with them. Jewish political, economic, social, religious and artistic life all bear witness to Muslim influence. It should be borne in mind that the language that the Jews spoke in Muslim lands was Arabic. Saadia Gaon, Bahya ibn Pakuda, Judah ha-Levi, and Maimonides all composed their philosophical works in Arabic. And this is the more easily understood when one remembers that it is to the Arabs that we owe the rediscovery of the philosophies of the classical age and their transmission, through Hebrew translations, to the Western world. Arabic was used by Jews for philosophic discourse not only because the major inspiration of their works was in Arabic, but also because Hebrew did not have the verbal resource or flexibility for such writing. It was only when the Jewish Arabic philosophical works were translated into Hebrew for the benefit of the non-Arabic speaking Jews of Provence and elsewhere, that the language of the Bible and the Mishna was given a new philosophical dimension. This was, in the main, the accomplishment of the Tibbonid family of translators.

The philosophy of the Arabs exerted a strong influence on the Jews. The poetry of the Arabs did likewise. This is not the place to enter into a detailed analysis of the forms and content of Arabic poetry. Suffice it to say that it brought to the Hebrew poetic mind the gifts of a quantitative metre, and of rhyme. It also brought a very refined and closely defined style. The adaptation of the Hebrew language to these new influences was both a laborious and a conscious process. Up to this time the poetry of the Jews was a poetry that relied on stress for its rhythm, not on the quantity of its syllables. For its structure it had depended on parallelism of expression, or on such artificial devices as the alphabetical acrostic, not on rhyme. The success of this complete transformation was mainly due to the pioneering work of Dunash ha-Levi ibn Labrat (tenth century), the major theorist among the early poets of the Spanish school, though the small amount of his poetry that has survived does not allow us to determine whether he succeeded in carrying out in practice the aims that he propounded.

We may well ask, however, why it was that the Jewish poets of Spain wrote in Hebrew at all. Why adapt Hebrew to a style that was foreign to it, when, just as they had done in the field of philosophy, they might have expressed themselves perfectly well in Arabic? They did, in fact, write some poems in Arabic, and the inscriptions to their Hebrew poems are more often than not in Arabic. But their choice of Hebrew for their poetry was due to two factors.

Firstly, a large amount of their poetic output was liturgical. Hebrew, although not the language of their daily lives, was the language of their faith. It was the language of their prayers, and the language of their study. Therefore, although striving to beautify their religion with poetry based upon Arabic models, they were not tempted to use the language of Islam in order to worship the God of the Jews.

Secondly, in the field of poetry, the Hebrew language did not suffer from the same inadequacies as were apparent in the domain of philosophy. On the contrary, Hebrew was at this very time experiencing a new lease of life. A Jewish sect, the Karaites, who traced their origins

4

back to the end of the eighth century, rejected Rabbinic law and appealed directly to the words of the Bible for the authority for their faith. Their opponents, the Rabbanites, of whom the most redoubtable was Saadia Gaon, were compelled to re-examine the literal meaning of Scripture in order to argue with the Karaites on their own ground. This led to a reopening of the Jewish mind and imagination to the actual words of the Bible, denuded of their traditional Rabbinic interpretation, and subject to the enquiries of grammarians and linguists, who used the cognate Arabic abundantly in order to clarify the meaning of the Hebrew word of God.

The Jews of Spain took part enthusiastically in this rediscovery of the Hebrew Bible. And when the intellectual hegemony of the Jews passed from the Academies of Sura and Pumbeditha in the East to the schools of Lucena and Cordoba in the West, Spanish Jews were in the forefront of those who sought primarily the literal significance of Scripture. So it was that the Jewish poets of Spain seized the opportunity to divest the Hebrew muse of the clumsy coinages and the obscure Talmudic connotations of the *payyetanim,* and used throughout only the 'pure' language of the Bible.

The phraseology of the Bible was put to use in every sort of context, from the most sensual love-song, to the greatest devotional utterance. There were some interpretations of the Bible which were everywhere current among Jews; for example, the use of Esau and Edom to represent the Roman and, later, the Christian, power, and the use of Ishmael and his scriptural descendants to symbolise Islam. Similarly, it was quite normal among Jews to see the 'Song of Songs' as a dialogue between God and Israel and, later, as a communion between man and his soul. One cannot over-emphasise the power, in Hebrew poetry of the Spanish period, of the innuendo, of the sudden glinting of a Biblical expression, of the new light shed on the meaning of a well-known phrase, and, throughout, of the profound insight and understanding that the poet brought to the Biblical text—an insight and an understanding which he wished to convey to his hearers and which he expected them to seize with immediate comprehension. Indeed, it might be said that, rather than the Bible enriching their poetry, their poetry enriched the Bible.

This is the greatest obstacle that the translator of this poetry and his non-Hebrew speaking reader have to encounter. We are no longer, for the most part, familiar with our Bible in English, let alone in Hebrew. And how is it possible for a reader unacquainted with all that the words of Scripture have meant for the learned religious Jew to grasp the import and subtlety of the poems written by the Jews of Spain? And yet, despite this difficulty, there is still something that may be communicated, and it is this that I have endeavoured to transmit.

The Jews of Spain followed their Arabic masters in much of their poetic subject-matter, but they often transmuted it into specifically Jewish material. (One remarkable example of this transmutation is that, whereas the Arabs wrote poems in praise of the cities of Spain, the Jews, using the same poetic phraseology as the Arabs, reserved their paeans for the glories of Israel and Jerusalem.) They wrote love-songs to individuals of both sexes; and how much of this material is conventional stylisation, and how much represents real physical experience it is difficult to say. Their poems describe wine-feasts that were held in the beautiful gardens of Spain, with girls in attendance, singing to stringed instruments. We find in their poetry extravagant praises of fellow-poets and of wealthy patrons. We find too sarcastic criticism. We share with them their sorrow at the departure of friends for distant lands, and at the deaths of their loved ones. We travel with them on their journeys, some enforced through persecution and banishment, others undertaken out of love for the land of Israel.

We encounter often their awareness of the passing of time, of the futility of life, of the precious quality of the immortal soul. And, above all, we experience with them their search for the knowledge of God, their sense of dependence on him as the Creator of the world, their consciousness of the relationship between God and the Jewish people, their desire to serve him with all their being, their remorse at their own iniquity, their torment and their bewilderment at the sufferings of their people.

Yet despite the similarity in content, each of the major poets is able to strike a personal note. We recognise Halevi's yearning for the land of Israel, Gabirol's communion with his own soul, Moses ibn Ezra's grief in his exile, and the extraordinary martial character of Samuel ha-Nagid. It is indeed this personal element which distinguishes the content of Spanish Hebrew poetry from that of the Hebrew poetry of medieval France and Germany.

The Spanish period not only saw the efflorescence for the first time since the 'Song of Songs' of secular Hebrew poetry. It also provided for the first time the framework for the professional Jewish poet. Many of the poets represented in this volume followed other callings in addition to their writing poetry. They were physicians, politicians, rabbis, and merchants. But others followed their Arab masters, and sought wealthy patrons. They were commissioned to write songs of praise to celebrate births or marriages, elegies to commemorate the dead. They were able, also, if they were offended, to satirise their masters, as well as eulogise them. And many are the poetic laments to be found describing the bad faith or the miserliness of the patron.

Critics of a previous generation might have been perturbed by the curious mixture of deep faith and unbridled sensuality which is to be found in the poetic output of the Spanish Jews. But to-day we see these poets in the wider context of medieval literature and we know that the medieval poet accepted the fact of the conflict between his religious aspirations and his sensual desires. Both sides of his nature find independent expression in his poetry. And the conflict between them is also frequently demonstrated in his poems themselves. Even the renunciation of youthful excesses which we find often among Jewish and Muslim poets, as they reached maturer years, may be paralleled in the literature of other peoples, from the earliest flowering of poetry in Christian Western Europe to the English Metaphysicals. Already among the poets of Spain, it was probably a poetic convention rather than a heartfelt confession. The love-poetry we find here is courtly and refined, and there is no room for the earthy or the bawdy.

It is not easy to say how much influence this poetry had on the growth of Western European literature. A controversy has raged for more than a century on the part that Arab poets played in the growth of the troubadour poetry of Provence. It seems very probable that the content and structure of Arab poetry made its way, through the Romance vernacular, to the poets of Southern France. Provencal troubadour poetry had its origin about the year 1100. And, although there is no precise evidence, one wonders whether the Hebrew poets might have had a share in the communication of poetic themes. A reader must be struck by the remarkable parallel between the many poems on the 'Ubi sunt' theme in the Western tradition, and similar poems in the same vein in the Hebrew tradition, some of which are represented in this collection. Perhaps the truth is simply that Muslim, Jew, and Christian shared these sentiments, and expressed their feelings independently. At all events, there seems to be room for more study of the extent to which the Jews may have been responsible for the transmission of poetic material from the Arabs to the Christians, in the same way as they were responsible for the transmission of philosophy.

The finest flowering of Spanish Hebrew poetry took place in the two centuries 1000-1200. After that time imitators arose in both Provence and Italy, but they did not approach the eminence of their forbears. Rather did they find their forte in the rhymed narrative, and the comic epigram.

A Note on the Translations

THE POETS REPRESENTED IN THIS VOLUME are considered here first and foremost as poets Whatever their philosophical standpoint, whatever the vicissitudes of their life-stories, and their political or spiritual significance, they are abused if their work is not presented as poetry. This therefore has been my first aim, and it is on this basis that I offer these translations to the public. If I have written bad poetry then I have done the poets a grave injustice.

A little has already been said concerning the large part played by biblical references in these poems. Occasionally, this comes over in the translation. It will be the more apparent to the reader who knows his Bible. From time to time, where I have thought that a reference to the Bible was essential to the understanding of a substantial point in the poem, I have drawn attention to it in the notes.

The making of poetry in Muslim lands was a far different exercise from the making of poetry to-day. It was predominantly an intellectual, formally precise, operation. The metres of the Arabs, adopted by the Jews, were complicated and varied. Rhyme-schemes likewise required the skill of an artist in mosaic for their perfection. Practically all their poems were rhymed. Because of the structure of the semitic languages, whose nouns have possessive suffixes, and whose verbs likewise are conjugated partly by the changing of word-endings, it was not a difficult matter for Jewish and Arab poets to write long poems based entirely on one rhyme. Thus, the war-epic of Samuel ha-Nagid 'The Victory over Ben Abbad' has 149 lines all ending in the masculine plural, *lim*. I have approached this problem in a thoroughly eclectic manner, rejecting the rhyme and metre of the original if I felt it would not contribute to, or would adversely affect, the poetic quality of the English translation; but imitating both rhyme and metre where I found this did not clash with, or really enhanced, the English rendering. I have found assonantal rhyme to be generally more serviceable than pure

9

rhyme. In all I have judged more by an English eye and ear rather than by a desire to be faithful to the Hebrew poetic structure.

Where the sense of the poem is concerned, however, I have endeavoured at all times to be faithful to the original. Where English usage has compelled me to diverge to any great extent from the Hebrew, I have always, I trust, given a literal rendering in the notes.

Every student of the Hebrew poetry of Spain is incalculably indebted to the scholars who have done pioneering work in presenting to the public from manuscripts and early printed prayer-books the rich legacy of the Hebrew imagination. I should like to express my particular gratitude to the works of H. Brody and H. Schirmann, especially to the two anthologies: *Mibchar ha-Shirah ha-'Ivrith* by Brody and Wiener, Leipzig, 1922; and *Ha-Shirah ha-'Ivrith bi-Sefarad u-bi-Provence* by H. Schirmann, Jerusalem-Tel-Aviv, 1956. I give references to both these anthologies in the notes. I am especially indebted to the many articles and notes of Schirmann, and have endeavoured always to record his name in the notes where I have particularly made use of his work.

Every generation needs to make for itself new translations of its foreign classics. The great majority of these poems appear in English here for the first time, but some of them, in particular Ha-Levi's 'Zion' poems, have had previous translators, and translations of other poems not included here have appeared. Those who wish to embark on a further reading are referred to the Bibliography. However, there is still a vast store of Hebrew poetry which would be worthy of translation into English.

Bibliography

Translations

SALAMAN, NINA, *Selected Poems of Jehuda Halevi*, 1924.

SOLIS-COHEN, *Selected Poems of Moses ibn Ezra*, 1923.

ZANGWILL, ISRAEL, *Selected Religious Poems of Solomon ibn Gabirol*, 1923. (These three form part of the Schiff Library of Jewish Classics, Philadelphia).

LUCAS, ALICE, *The Jewish Year*, Routledge, 1926.

LEWIS, BERNARD, *The Kingly Crown*, Vallentine Mitchell, 1961. (This is a translation of Gabirol's *Keter Malchuth*. I have not included therefore any selections from that poem here.)

HALPER, *Post-Biblical Hebrew Literature*, Philadelphia, Vol. I (Texts) 1946, Vol. II (Translations) 1948.

Literary Background

WAXMAN, *A History of Jewish Literature*, New York, new edition, 1960.

HAZM, IBN, *The Ring of the Dove*, trans. A. R. Nykl, Paris, 1931.

NYKL, A. R., *Hispano-Arabic Poetry and its Relationship with the Provencal Troubadours*, Baltimore, 1941.

Historical Background

BROCKELMANN, CARL, *History of the Islamic Peoples*, Routledge, 1952.

HITTI, *The History of the Arabs*, Macmillan, 1956.

BAER, YIZHAK, *History of the Jews in Christian Spain*, Philadelphia, 1961.

MARGOLIS and MARX, *History of the Jewish People*, Philadelphia, 1947.

NEUMAN, A. A., *The Jews in Spain*, Philadelphia, 1944.

DUNASH HA-LEVI BEN LABRAT

DUNASH HA-LEVI BEN LABRAT came from a distinguished
Jewish family of the Eastern Caliphate, and was, according
to Moses ibn Ezra, born in Fez, in Morocco, in the first half
of the tenth century. He studied under the great Jewish
grammarian and philosopher, Sa'adia Gaon, in Baghdad,
returned to Fez after Sa'adia's death (942), and later attached
himself to the family of Hasdai ibn Shaprut in Cordoba.

It was Dunash who first demonstrated both in theory and
in practice how Hebrew could be adapted to the writing of
poetry in imitation of Arabic usage. His fame as a gram-
marian, and as a poet, quickly spread throughout the Jewish
communities of Spain. Only a few of his poems have
survived. The date of his death is unknown.

Reply to an Invitation
to a Feast

He said: 'Do not sleep.
Drink vintage wine,
While henna and lily,
Myrrh and aloes,

Pomegranates and dates,
Tamarisks and grapes,
And pleasant anemones
Fill the garden rows.

The singers are accompanied
By cithern and viol,
The ripple of the fountains,
The murmur of the lute.

All the little birds
Sing among the leaves,
In the tall trees,
Whose boughs are thick with fruit.

The doves are moaning
As if thinking of music,
And the pigeons answer
With flute-like tones.

We shall drink in the gardens
Surrounded by lilies,
And with songs of praise
Ease our weary bones.

We shall eat sweetmeats
And drink from bowls,
Pretend we are giants,
And drink from the vats.

I shall go out to the herd
And kill some fine beasts,
Both calves and rams,
All choice and fat.

We shall pour out fine oil,
Burn woody spices.
Let us finish our feast
Before life's last hour!'

I rebuked him: 'Silence!
How can you talk so,
When the Temple, God's footstool,
Is in the enemy's power?

Your words are foolish.
You prefer to be idle.
Your thoughts are worthless.
You scorn the divine.

You no longer think
On the law of God.
You can be happy,
And there are foxes in Zion.

How can we drink wine?
How raise our eyes?
When we are as nothing,
A race all despise!'

A Song for the Sabbath

He will proclaim freedom for all his sons,
And will keep you, as the apple of his eye.
Pleasant is your name, and will not be destroyed.
Repose, relax, on the Sabbath day.

Seek my portals and my home.
Give me a sign of deliverance.
Plant a vine in my vineyard.
Look to my people, hear their laments.

Tread the wine-press in Bozrah,
And in Babylon, that city of might.
Crush my enemies in anger and fury.
On the day when I cry, hear my complaint.

Place, O God, in the mountain waste,
Fir and acacia, myrtle and elm.
Give those who teach, and those who obey,
Abundant peace, like the flow of a stream.

Repel my enemies, O zealous God.
Fill their hearts with fear and despair.
Let us open our mouths, let us fill
Our tongues with praise for your power.

Know wisdom, that your soul may live,
And this shall be a diadem for your brow.
Keep the commandment of your Holy One.
Observe your Sabbath, your sacred day.

JOSEPH IBN ABITHUR

JOSEPH IBN ABITHUR was born in the middle of the tenth century in Merida. He lived in Cordoba which was the centre of Muslim and Jewish civilisation in Spain at this time. There is a tradition, preserved by Abraham ibn Daoud, that he gave an Arabic explanation of the Talmud to the Caliph al-Hakim II.

Joseph was surrounded by controversy. He was forced to leave Spain after making an unsuccessful bid for the intellectual leadership of the Jewish community, and he spent the latter part of his life journeying in the lands of the Middle East. He died in Damascus after 1012.

He is known as a poet mainly for his liturgical work, much of which was adopted into the prayer-books of the Provencal, Catalonian, and North African Jews. In the main his poetry is more akin to that of the *piyyutim* of Eastern Mediterranean Jewry than to the 'new' poetry beginning to flourish in Spain.

Sanctification

In the heights of heaven is the throne of your dwelling,
And among the earth-bound is your dominion's strength.
These praise your glorious majesty,
And these sanctify your kingdom's name.
There is none holy like the Lord, for there is none beside you.

In the heights of heaven is his throne of praise,
And the hem of his train fills his Temple.
Some on his left side and some on his right,
The seraphim stand all about him.

Among the earth-bound, acknowledged God's people,
They are standing to-day like poor petitioners,
Praising and thanking the Rock who redeems.
They hallow Jacob's Holy One, the God of Israel.

In the heights of heaven, the exalted angels
Emerge with fear, and return in trembling,
And greet in terror the King, the only One,
Six wings to each and every being.

Among the earth-bound, all the congregations
Approach to-day with their five prayers.
They sanctify God with a sound of roaring,
And you, the Holy One, dwell among praises.

In the heights of heaven God's name is complete.
Each heart springs up, all flesh bristles.
One troop cries ' Where? ' to the other,
And each calls to the other, and proclaims.

Among the earth-bound are the choice of the holy ones,
Possessors of the engraved law, clinging to his name.
The Lord of Hosts arises with a strong hand,
And the Holy God is rightfully hallowed.

In the heights of heaven are angels of the hosts,
And among the earth-bound, ponderers on the prophet's law.
These glorify with tumultuous shouting,
And these sanctify in hundreds and thousands:
Holy, holy, holy is the Lord of Hosts !

A Song for the New Year

Who established the heavens on high? Who stretched out the
    sphere of the stars?
Which god is great like God? Who can speak of the divine
    powers?
Before you, O God, praise is dumb.

Who spoke and his word prevailed, when he spread out his skies?
Who ordered and his order stood, when he disposed his world?
Who put boundaries round the seas, when he determined their
    lines?
Who joined the clods of the earth when he constructed its
    valleys?
Who fixed the earth's dimensions? Do you know?
    Who held the rule?

Who puts on a robe of glory, and wraps himself in honour?
In whose memory is righteousness, whose ways are humility?
Who is the powerful God, full of strength, before whom the
    lofty bow?
Who utters mysteries, and proclaims them by word of mouth?
Who speaks, and it happens, without the Lord's command?

Who threw the breakers into the depths of the sea?
Who spaces each wave at three hundred leagues?
Who utters a word to pierce a channel for the rain?
Who brings each drop from its own mould to promote
    fertility?
Who gathers the wind in his hands? Who takes up the sea in
    his garment?

Who counts the ninety-nine groans of the mountain-goat?
Who trains the eagle to take her young on its wings as it flies?
Who supplies the snake to bite the hinds as they bear?
Who makes for each thunder-clap a separate path through
    the sky?
Who pierces a channel for the rain, a way for the lightning bolt?

Who prepares the hair for the head of man as he grows?
Who arranges each one in its place, so his life is untrammeled?
Who beautifies every being like the first man's glory?
Who likens the child to the father in shape, in speech, in voice?
Who will tell him how to go? Who will requite him for his acts?

Who casts five terrors on the five giants of the world?
Who instils in the massive elephant dread of the gnat?
Who inflames fear of the stickleback in the hidden leviathan?
Who speaks and shows that he is ruler of them all?
Who can oppose him and still be at peace?

Who causes the destroyer to burst irresistibly upon the strong?
Who brings the sudden fly of Ethiopia to terrify the lion?
Who arouses the scorpion's fear of the paltry spider?
Who draws out the eagle's anguish for the swallow in the sky?
Who establishes the limits of the world?

Lament on the Devastation
of the Land of Israel (1012)

Weep, my brothers, weep and mourn
Over Zion with great moan,
Like the lament of Hadadrimmon,
Or of Josiah, son of Amon.

Weep for the tender and delicate ones
Who barefoot now tread upon thorns,
Drawing water for barbarians,
Felling trees at their commands.

Weep for the man who is oppressed,
In bondage inexperienced.
They say to him: "Carry! Make haste!"
And he, among burdens, finds no rest.

Weep for the fathers when they see
Their sons, none more praiseworthy,
Whose price gold cannot buy,
At the hands of Cushites condemned to die.

Weep for the blind who wander on,
Defiled, through the land of Zion,
With the blood of pregnant women,
The blood of the aged and young children.

Weep for the pious, whom the unclean goad,
Force them to eat forbidden food,
To make them forget their bond with God,
And the land, where their joys reside.

Weep for the women pure and chaste,
Whose fidelity had never ceased,
Subject to Hamitic lust,
Conceiving, with terror in their breast.

Weep for the daughters, noble
And upright as sculptured marble,
Forced to be slaves to the ignoble,
Who are themselves a servile rabble.

Weep. Weep and mourn
The synagogues forlorn,
That wild beasts have torn down,
And desert birds have made their own.

Weep for those in the enemies' grip,
Gathered together for a day without hope,
For those poor souls who have drained the cup,
Who are suffering now murder and rape.

Weep, weep for our living.
Do not weep for our dying;
For, as long as we have being,
To be like the dead is our desiring.

Therefore, my friend, do not recall
Consolation for my soul,
For those torn in pieces, all
In Zion, with no burial.

ISAAC IBN KALPON

ISAAC IBN KALPON came from a North African Jewish family, was born in the middle of the tenth century, lived a while in Cordoba, and spent a great deal of his life wandering from one city to another.

His poems are full of complaints against his patrons and contemporaries. He had a firm friend however in his considerably younger contemporary, Samuel ha-Nagid. He died some time after 1020.

A Present of Cheese

I invited you, my dearest friend, with joy,
And heaped upon you favours, as my guest.
I regarded you as a shield and a buckler
Against my enemies, a tower of strength, my trust—
Like a hut in the shade when the sun beats down,
Like a warm stove in time of snow and frost.
I remembered you—and may God remember you for good—
As Elkanah remembered Peninah—with the best.
And you send me a present, a portion of cheese.
And what's the good of cheese, when I am dry with thirst?

SAMUEL HA-NAGID

OF ALL THE POETS represented in this collection, Samuel
ha-Nagid has the most remarkable life-story. According to
his own testimony, he felt himself at an early age destined to
reach great heights in the political life of Spain. He was, at
one and the same time, poet, rabbi, statesman, and general,
and distinguished in each one of these fields. His poems are
some of the finest in the whole range of Hebrew literature.
His expertise in the elucidation of Biblical and rabbinic litera-
ture was acknowledged by all. His political astuteness was
immensely valuable to his Muslim rulers. His generalship
was rewarded with victory in war.

Samuel ha-Levi ben Joseph ibn Nagrela was born in
Cordoba in 993. After the invasion of the North African
Berbers in 1013, he was forced to leave Cordoba, which was
sacked, and he settled in Malaga, which was, at this time,
part of the Berber province of Granada. The story goes that,
while in Malaga, his skill as an Arabic calligraphist came to
the attention of the vizier Abu al-Kasim ibn al-Arif, and he
was appointed the latter's private secretary. Before the vizier
died, he recommended Samuel to Habbus, king of Granada,
who made him vizier in 1027. The Jews henceforth called
him *Nagid* (Prince) as a mark of his eminence within the
Jewish community.

When Habbus died, Samuel was among those who
favoured the claims of the older prince, Badis, and on the
latter's accession he was rewarded by being appointed vizier,
and commander of the king's armies. In this capacity he
fought often against the armies of Seville. Indeed, between
1038 and 1056 there were only two years when he was not
involved in some military conflict. His son Joseph appears to
be the only other Jew to have commanded a Muslim army.
Samuel died in 1056 in Granada.

His poems are noteworthy for the way in which he was
able to inform the artificiality and occasional preciosity of
construction with deep and obviously sincere content. His
long martial poems are unique in the poetic output of the
Spanish Jews.

In Praise of Wine

Red in appearance, sweet to the taste,
Vintage of Spain, yet renowned in the East,
Feeble in the cup, but, once up in the brain,
It rules over heads that cannot rise again.

The mourner, whose blood is mixed with his tears—
The blood of the grape demolishes his fears.
Friends, passing the cup from hand to hand,
Seem to be gambling for a precious diamond.

An Invitation

My friend, tell me,
When shall I pour you my wine?
The cry of the cock woke me,
And sleep has deserted my eyes.

Come out and see the morning light
Like a scarlet thread in the East.
Make haste, give me a cup,
Before the dawn starts to rise,

Of spiced pomegranate juice
From the perfumed hand of a girl,
Who will sing songs. My soul
Revives and then dies.

The Power of the Pen

Man's wisdom is at the tip of his pen,
His intelligence is in his writing.
His pen can raise a man to the rank
That the sceptre accords to a king.

On the Death of His Brother

Alas, I return with an anguished spirit.
(May God have mercy on you, my brother!)
I buried you, one day ago;
On this day too, my thoughts are bitter.
I bear you greetings. Do you not hear
When I call out to you with all my power?
Answer me. Do you not recognise
The sound of my lamenting prayer?
Are your teeth becoming slack in the jaw?
Are your bones now beginning to wither?
Has your moistness disappeared in the night,
As mine has fled through the tears of a mourner?
I have left you, my father's first-born,
A solemn pledge in the hand of my Maker.
I know that you will go in peace
To him who gives knowledge to the believer.

II

The days of my mourning are now at an end.
Yet the days of my sorrow are not complete.
Throughout the days and nights of my grief
My body laments in throes of anguish.
Alas, alas, what sorrow is mine,
How bitter my life, what grief is there,
For my own brother, my mother's son,
My forehead's diadem and my perfection.
Is this the fate that I must suffer?

How is it that this has befallen me?
How was it possible that in my majesty
And high estate mine should be the voice of woe?
If an enemy had taken hold of him,
I should have repelled him with all my strength.
If a large ransom could bring him back,
I should redeem him with all my wealth.
But, now, to-day, what can I do?
For such is the ordinance of my God.

III

Is there a sea between me and you
That I should not turn to bear you greeting?
That I should not run with a fearful heart,
That I should not sit by the side of your grave?
In truth, if I were not to do this
I should be a traitor to your brotherly love.
Alas, my brother, here am I sitting
Facing you, at the side of your grave,
And there is in my heart grief for you,
Like the day when your death first caused me to grieve.
And now if I come with the greeting of "Peace!"
I shall not hear the answer you give.
And you will not come out to meet me
When I come to visit the land that you own.
You will not be glad when I approach,
And I cannot be glad when I am near you.
You will not be able to see my face,
And I shall never see your like again;
Because in Sheol is now your home,
And your residence is in the grave.
My father's first-born, my mother's son,
May you have peace in your last existence.
May the spirit of God rest upon you,
Upon your soul, upon your spirit.

I shall go now to my land, for
In the earth have they enclosed you.
I shall sleep a while and wake a while,
And you will slumber eternally.
And until the day when I too change,
The fire of your parting will remain in my heart.

Man Runs towards the Grave

Man runs towards the grave,
And rivers hasten to the great deep.
The end of all living is their death,
And the palace in time becomes a heap.
Nothing is further than the day gone by,
And nothing nearer than the day to come,
And both are far, far away
From the man hidden in the heart of the tomb.

The Old Man's Warning

You laugh at me, now that you are young,
Because you see me old, and grey-haired.
I am an old man, but I have seen workmen
Make a coffin and a bier for a young lad.

The Hour in which I am

She said to me: 'Rejoice, that God has brought you
To the age of fifty in this world.' She was not aware
That there is no difference to me between my days
That have passed and what I hear of the days of Noah.
There is nothing for me in the world but the hour in which I am.
It lasts but a moment, and, like a cloud, is no more.

Two Bouts of Woe

Consider how shameful rejoicing is,
Since it comes between two bouts of woe.
You wept when you came into this world,
And another will mourn you when you go.

I Look up to the Sky

I look up to the sky and the stars,
And down to the earth and the things that creep there.
And I consider in my heart how their creation
Was planned with wisdom in every detail.
See the heavens above like a tent,
Constructed with loops and with hooks,
And the moon with its stars, like a shepherdess
Sending her sheep into the reeds;
The moon itself among the clouds,
Like a ship sailing under its banners;
The clouds like a girl in her garden
Moving, and watering the myrtle-trees;
The dew-mist—a woman shaking
Drops from her hair to the ground.
The inhabitants turn, like animals, to rest,
(Their palaces are their stables);
And all fleeing from the fear of death,
Like a dove pursued by the falcon.
And these are compared at the end to a plate
Which is smashed into innumerable sherds.

The Citadel

I stationed a strong force in a citadel
Which soldiers had destroyed long ago.
We slept there, in it, and around it,
And its owners slept beneath us, down below.

I said to myself: 'Where are the people,
Those who lived here in years that have gone?
Where are the builders and destroyers, the slaves,
And their masters, the princes and the woe-begone?

Where are the parents, the bereaved, the fathers,
The sons, the bridegrooms, and the mourners,
And the large numbers that were born after these,
As the seasons turned through the cycle of the years?

They were all neighbours on the face of the earth,
And now they lie together in the earth's womb.
They moved to the dust from their pleasant courts,
And from their palaces towards the tomb.

Were they to raise their heads and emerge,
They would despoil us, of our lives and possessions.
In truth, my soul, in truth, by to-morrow,
I shall be like them, and all my companions.'

God's Assurance

On a day of danger and distress I remember your message.
You are good, and there is justice in your mouth and your heart.
I remember the message which comes to console me
When sorrow appears. I put faith in your help.
When your servant in his youth lay asleep in his bed, you sent
Seraphim to tell him of your great goodness.
They sat down beside me, and then Michael said:
'This is God's message who pleads your cause:
"On the day that you cross waters of sorrow I am with you.
When the enemy draws near, the rivers will not drown you".'

And Gabriel, too, his companion, who has heard
Of your chariot, and all that surrounds you, said to me:
'When you walk into the fire, it shall not burn you.
I shall speak to the flames, and they will never destroy you.'
This is the message on which I rely like a sword in the hand.
I see swords before me. I trust in your sword.

The Victory over Ben Abbad

Will you perform for me every year deeds
Like those you executed for the princes and patriarchs?
Will you slaughter lions for me instead of goats,
And offer them instead of ewes for sacrifice?
Shall I every year pass through the heart of the sea
And will the breakers be turned into highways?
Shall I every year walk through the fire
And will you change its flames into shade for me?
You, my rock, you it is right to praise.
You are God, and from your hand comes power.
You seduce the cowards at their last hour,
And, in the day of vengeance, you remove the dross.
I shall tell of your glory in the gates
And give thanks to your name in the congregations.
I shall recount your marvels in the assembly of the pious,
And your wonders among those who wear fringes.

About a year ago, on a day of terror like this,
You redeemed me, and made the wicked my ransom.
Now that Ben Abbas has met his death,
So Ben Abbad approaches and fear takes hold of me.
Both have pursued me, but the first was a common man,
While on this one's head sits the crown of majesty.
It is at his command that the nobility ascend
To the court, and at his word they are sent away.
By his permission the mighty take possession
Of their lands. They are executed at his desire.
The captains of the Berbers obey his voice.
He is praised by the princes of Ishmael.
They look to his command as to the first shower;
They are expectant for his thought as for the rain.

There is strife and hatred between him and my king.
Each rules his land far from the other.
Both are like cedars among the kings,
And all the earth's monarchs are mere saplings.
Both have learnt how to hunt kings.
The mighty are consumed by their swords.
They have pierced crowned heads like paupers,
And have sacrificed the great like rams.
No one in Spain can stand against them
To disregard their commands or raise rebellion.

Then he set out to wage a trial of strength
And arrayed his armies upon the frontiers.
He took a city and a kingdom in his path,
And there was none to prevent him, none to protest.
In the face of his forces lords became slaves.
Fear of him made weaklings of the strong.
His army numbered chieftains in thousands,
Advancing in columns beneath their banners.

In their own land they were evil men, making
The children of the living God suffer their reproaches.
They conspired against them, seized
Weapons, and brought shackles for their feet,
To destroy the mothers in Israel, the men,
The sucklings, and those newly weaned.

And when the heart of their king grew haughty
And he spoke with pride, we laughed at him.
We crossed over into his land in strength
To revenge ourselves on our despoiled princes.
Warriors went with us like savage lions,
And a multitude like a swarm of locusts.
The soldiers were unhindered by superfluous flesh,
Nor by flabbiness on their loins.
All girded their swords in that day of wrath,
And stripped off their cloaks to join battle.

All hastened towards the sword, running
To the slaughter, in good heart and in joy,
In coats of mail, shimmering like the waves,
And with shields, red as rolled parchment,
With brow-plates, and round helmets,
Upon horses swift and darting as the clouds.
The soldiers' hands held no lances, nor spears,
As if they themselves were tough as tamarisks.
You would see nothing but the glint of a sling-stone.
You would hear nothing but the cries of delight.

We returned after the slaughter and the burning,
And our hands were full of the spoils of war.
His messengers returned to him with words
Like silver dross, or wine mixed with water.
They misled him with their exaggerations and their lies,
As if they were plotting against his life.
God consumed the advice of his captains
And considered their discernment to be that of babes.
After we had come back, they said to him:
'Will you sit in this fortress and not pursue them as they fall?
Should you not go out to despoil your exhausted foes?
Should you not hasten to cut down these stragglers?'
And he left in haste to give pursuit, as they said,
With hundreds and thousands of infantrymen.
They arrayed themselves on the bank of the river,
And against them stood their enemy as at the battle of the
          ravine.
They stood, ready, arrayed for the battle,
Shouting with war-like strength like the pipes.
You could not liken them to the warriors
Of dead Agag, nor compare their weapons.
Those who knew them in the past realised they were
No more than women, but these were their male warriors.
When they rode, they ran like wild asses,
And their footsoldiers, like harts and stags.
Their armour was like the armour of royalty,

48

With ornamented robes, and crowns for their heads.
In their strength, their number, and their power
They provide poets with their metaphors.

When I saw this army so superior
To the slaughtered and reviled force of Amalek,
When I saw great warriors afraid
And the mighty men of battle trembling,
Captains going to war with reluctance
And princes refusing to take up the fight;
When I remembered the enemy's purpose
Against my puny and weakling people,
The foes already sharing their spoil
And casting lots over the captured land;
When I saw death's first-born before me,
And soldiers taking leave of their lives in the battle;
Then I raised my hand in the name of God,
The honoured, the awesome, acclaimed by his seventy armies.
At this time of distress I mentioned his name in my heart,
To implore thereby him who dwells in the skies,
To overcome the power of the foe with the force of
        the Rock,
For he can take an army in the palm of his hand.
And, at such a time, the patriarchs, with prayers
For mercy, entreat for me the grace of almighty God.
With the winding-rope of prayer, together they raise
And draw up salvation from the dust.
In their perfection and their righteousness, they speak
Words of truth, and restrain and imprison his anger.

The Lord is mine. He said: 'Trust in me.
And I shall make your steps fall in pleasant places.
I shall smash for you the teeth of the lions.
I shall strike down before you the sons of the giants.'
Then he donned his garment of wrath and went out,
As on the day of Pharaoh and his drowned army.

He revealed himself, not by a window or in secret,
And he looked down openly, not from behind a wall.
He exalted himself above my enemies. They were like
Chaff from a threshing-floor, and rotted there like leaves.
He played havoc with them, and made them dance
Like the young of an ox, like a kid, like a calf.

He made them forget their strength.
They were like women and young children.
He sent an angel who deflected their weapons,
And turned their right-hands into left-hands.
He sent an angel who distorted their counsel,
And turned their strategists into fools.
He put lies in the mouth of their scouts, their captains,
        and their messengers,
To mete out to them the death of the impious.

When they saw what it was that pursued them,
Then they took flight in seven different directions.
This was truly the work of God who turned
Their reward into the reward of idiots.
He tied ropes around their hands
And cords were bound across their hearts.
Their chariots were their own stumbling-blocks,
And their steeds were like chains on their feet.
He cut them off with the breath of his mouth
As a weaver snaps a cord. He broke them like threads.
I saw men of renown bound as prisoners,
And brought in, in fetters, dragged
Before the king. Some lived at his command.
Some at his request were slain.
I grew weary of seeing the smiting and the smitten,
Bespattered, immersed in the blood of life,
And the sole of the foot that had not yet touched
Ground, now wounded with thorns,
And warriors, stricken, pierced to the death,
Thrown to one side, corpses of the heathen.

On the night of the sixth day we pursued them
Like a ravening bird, like a swarm of bees.
We struck down their mighty men and their king;
Their captains and their servants were dead men.
They were like filth upon the face of the earth,
And their heads were in the dust like dung.
They exchanged their rooms, wide halls,
And porticoes, for the wild woods.
We captured our captors, and those that thought
To destroy us were themselves destroyed.
They imagined that we should be their possession,
But they themselves were possessed by our hands.

They put their trust in bows and lances,
And we were saved by the name of the mightiest among
       the mighty.
All those are now confounded who took for pledges
The shoes and garments of God's people.
They have seen the glorious deeds of the awesome One
Who requites in full those who plan evil.
He made his decision to destroy in his wrath
Their giants, like natural abortions.
Their nobles were no more than worms to him
In his anger, and their armies were as ants.

I have seen you, and you roar like a lion.
You annihilate lions with your roaring.
I have looked upon you; you rise up, you cry aloud,
You trumpet, you scatter the warriors.
You were revealed. The inner parts of my enemies
Groaned like the moaning of lutes.
You were angry. And I saw kings unable
To withstand your ire and your wrath.
They were eager for the battle before they saw us.
And when they saw us you made them impotent.
You turned their bows into so much straw,
And their arrows into useless gravel.

On the second day judgement was begun, and on the fifth
You appointed judges for my cause against them.
And as the shadows turned so you turned in your servant's
Cause against the Arab and the Berber.
And you saved the son of Abraham, in the month
Of the flowing rivers, from the worshippers of idols.
And after the departure of the ninety-ninth year,
Salvation grew for him like a plant from the earth.
You were a refuge for me, you preserved me
From the foe, from the hosts of the profane.
You stretched out your right hand for me in salvation,
And against my enemies in painful blows.
The angels of evil and destruction, who cause
Earth and heaven to tremble, were given their commands.
They threw upon them weapons of fury like the rain,
And wrath like drops from a storm-cloud.
You gave your servant the cup of salvation to drink
And to his enemies the cup that made them reel.

When the night of the eve of Gathering came,
Then all my darkened paths were made bright,
Like the night of Abram, and the night of Moses,
Joshua's noon-day, and the night when the siege was raised.
And I kept with correctitude the festivals of God,
According to the way of the dwellers in tents:
Sabbath-day, and Shofar-day, and Yom Kippur,
The days of Succoth, to the end of the pilgrims' feasts.
The fear of profanation was like a fire in my heart,
Even though you will find some less rigorous.
And God arranged, when work was forbidden,
That the armies were able to rest from their toil.

I shall make for God song upon song,
Because of the wonders which he has redoubled.
He pours scorn upon the scorners, and fulfils
The desires of the toilers and the humble.
I shall declare his praises, and relate them

To a rescued people, the exiled and the wanderers,
Although not all the inhabitants of earth and sky
Are able to praise his name because of this.

As the people brought to their succoth
Myrtle from the rocks, and branches from the palm,
The Rock raised me in his palm, and his tent
Concealed me, like a barred fortress.
And as they brought their willow, he made the desert
Into a city with walls and barricades for his servant's son.
He cut down my enemies' glory, as the people cut
The produce from the fine fruit trees.
And the leaves from the boughs were to a one
For my soul like a sacrifice or like the half-shekel.
He exalted himself by the waters for a people
Who arise with four kinds that grow by the waters.
As my enemies approached to eat my flesh
I arose, and they fell, their strength depleted.
They pained my heart, but God sent balm
For the time of torment and sorrow.
He gave orders to his ministering angels,
And they came, descending and ascending, to my help from
   the skies.
And upon the nation who thought to share his people's spoil
He apportioned calamities in his anger.

We shall build our succoth with joy,
And they will mourn their catastrophe.
We shall utter psalms of praise with delight,
And they will sing dirges of lamentation.

Was this done for me?—and I a worm, and no man,
Despised among the peoples, condemned among the lowly?
What am I, what is my life, my God?
I am great with sin, a man of evil deeds.
I am too small and undeserving
Of all the victories and the benefits performed for me.

And if you repay me in this world for my merits,
And give me recompense for my faith,
How shall I stand in the day of judgement?
How shall my guilt and my sin be forgiven?

To the God of strength, who appears in the storm-cloud,
And in the whirlwind against the keepers of idols,
Who has not given his glory to others,
Nor transferred his praise to images,
To him I have already composed a song;
And now this song of praise that is bright like the stars,
Like the style of its sister, well-set in lines,
According to the number of the psalmist's praises.
Their content is more precious than pearls,
And each verse well-ordered and weighed.
The mother of poetry is too barren to bear
Songs like it, and the fathers of poetry are bereaved.
Both of them all the days of my life shall be
Bracelets on my arm, and rings in my ears.
On the day of judgement they will speak for me
With words that drip myrrh and aloes.

Sons of my people, sing with me this poem of praise
Placed at the head of all panegyrics.
See that its words are ordered correctly
In the mouth of old men and of children.
And when in the future your sons ask
What it is, then you will reply:
'A song of praise to God who redeemed his friend,
Who composed it for the redeemed to recite.
It is a song of praise, great and glorious,
For the God of glory, and his great deeds.'

A Message to his Son, Joseph, on the Raising of the Siege of Lorca

Send a carrier-pigeon, although she cannot speak,
With a tiny letter attached to her wings,
Sweetened with saffron-water, perfumed with frankincense.
And when she rises to fly away, send with her another,
So that, should she meet an eagle, or fall into a snare,
Or fail to make haste, the second will speed away.
And when she comes to Joseph's house, she will coo on the
  roof-top.
When she flies down to his hand, he will rejoice in her, like a
  song-bird.
He will spread out her wings, and read a letter there:
'Know, my son, that the cursed band of rebels has fled,
Scattered among the hills like chaff from a windswept field,
And among the byways like sheep astray with no shepherd.
They looked to defeat their enemy but they did not see it.
As we went to destroy them, at that very hour they fled.
They were slaughtered, falling upon each other at the crossing.
Their designs against the barred, walled city were frustrated.
They were humiliated like thieves caught in the act.
They covered themselves with ignominy as with a garment.
Calamity attached itself to them like the skin to one's face.
They drank contempt from the beaker, and found the cup made
  them drunk.

In my heart there was the pain of a woman bearing her first child,
And God put balm upon it, like rain in the drought.

Then my eyes were brightened, and my enemies' plunged in
     gloom.
I sing with a joyful heart, and they utter only laments.
The voice of gladness is in my house, and their's hears
     bitter weeping.

To you, my rock and my tower, to you my soul sings.
When I was in trouble, my plaint was laid before you.
My son, put your heart in the glorious hand of my God.
Arise, sing my song in the full assembly of the people.
And make it an amulet to be bound on your hand,
And let it be written with pen of iron in your heart.'

War

War at first is like a young girl
With whom every man desires to flirt.
And at the last it is an old woman.
All who meet her feel grieved and hurt.

Israel, Arise

Terminate your reign, wicked queen.
Sarah, the despised, rule over your enemies.
Gazelle of Senir, your slumber has been long
On your bed of pain. Awake, arise.
Raise yourself; there is reward for your righteousness.
Cure yourself; there is balm for your injuries.

The Wounded Lion

At times of distress, strengthen your heart,
Even if you stand at death's door.
The lamp has light before it is extinguished.
The wounded lion still knows how to roar.

SOLOMON IBN GABIROL

WITH SOLOMON IBN GABIROL we leave the arena of war and politics and enter into a world of personal communion with the soul. He was born in Malaga in 1021 or 1022, and lived the greater part of his life in Saragossa. From his early years he was crippled by disease, and his illness is a constant theme of his poetry. He was compelled to live by his writing, and found a sympathetic patron in Yekutiel ben Isaac ibn Hasan, who was executed however in 1039. He was also, for a time, on friendly terms with Samuel ha-Nagid. Perhaps as a result of his indisposition, and his consequent sense of inferiority, he was not an easy companion, and he left Saragossa, to die, perhaps in Valencia, between 1053 and 1058.

He devoted much of his life to the pursuit of philosophy or 'wisdom', in which he found consolation for his physical cares. He was an adherent of the Neoplatonic school. His major work 'The Fountain of Life' had great influence in medieval Christian circles in its Latin form ('Fons Vitae'), and because of its lack of reference to traditional Jewish sources was not attributed to him, until Solomon Munk, in the nineteenth century, discovered a Hebrew version of the work which indicated his authorship. His absorption in the 'new' philosophy also contributed no doubt to his personal unpopularity in the Jewish community of Saragossa.

His fame as a poet rests mainly on his liturgical poems which are masterpieces of concision and delicacy, and on his long philosophical poem 'The Kingly Crown'. It was he who introduced into the Hebrew poetic canon the poem addressed to the 'soul', by which he generally meant man's intellectual aspiration to discover God.

An Apple for Isaac

My lord, take this delicacy in your hand.
Perceive its scent. Forget your longing.
On both sides it blushes, like a young girl
At the first touch of my hand on her breast.
An orphan it is without father or sister,
And far away from its leafy home.
When it was plucked, its companions were jealous,
Envied its journey, and cried aloud:
'Bear greetings to your master, Isaac.
How lucky you are to be kissed by his lips!'

The Writing of Winter

The winter writes with the ink of its rain and its showers,
With the nib of its lightning, with the hand of its clouds,
A message upon the garden, of violet and purple.
No human being can perform acts such as these.
And when the earth becomes jealous of the skies,
It embroiders its garments with flowers like the stars.

In Mourning for Yekutiel

See the sun redden in the evening
As if she had put on a scarlet robe.
She strips the north and south of colour,
And the west she clothes in purple.
And the earth—she leaves it naked,
Cowering in the shadow of night.
The skies darken, dressed in black,
In mourning for Yekutiel.

On the Death of Rab Hai

Weep, my people, put on sackcloth and sorrow,
Break all the instruments of music and song,
For Rab Hai, our master, the last remnant
Left to us in the world, has gone.
What shall we bemoan and lament first of all,
And for what shall we first grieve and mourn?
For the ark which now lies hidden in Zion,
Or for Rab Hai, buried in Babylon?

Separation from the Torah

You enquire gracefully of a man sick at heart,
'Why do you wear sackcloth and put ashes on your head?'
I do not mourn or grieve for someone that has died,
For every man dies. He gives no ransom instead.
But I am grief-stricken, because, being ill,
I cannot go to hear the Sefer Torah read.

His Illness

Forgive, my God, and overlook my sins,
Although one cannot fathom their number or their depth.
Remember, for my sake, your kindness, Lord,
And do not look at this sum of dust and earth.
Even if the decree has gone out against my life,
Annul it, my God, make it of no effect.
Consider my illness as my redemption.
Let my pain be my atonement and my death.

In the Morning I Look for You

In the morning I look for you,
My rock and my tower.
I lay my prayers before you,
That day and night are in me.

Before your greatness, I stand,
And am unnerved,
Because your eye will see
The thoughts that are in me.

What is it that the heart
Or the tongue can do,
And what power is there
In the spirit that is in me?

But I know you are pleased
With the songs that men make,
And so I shall praise you
While the divine soul is in me.

The Unity of God

All that is created, above and below,
Witness, declare, all as one:
'The Lord is One, and his name One.'

Thirty-two paths make up your way.
All that perceive them tell your greatness.
And they know that all is yours,
That you are God, the King, alone.

Their hearts ponder the created world.
They find all, save you, is more than one.
In number, in weight, all is measured.
All derives from one Master, alone.

From end to end there are signs of you,
North and west and east and south,
Sky and earth, your true witness,
On this side one, on that side one.

From you emanates the world entire.
You remain; the rest will perish.
And so all creation glorifies you,
For from beginning to end, the Father is One.

ISAAC IBN GI'AT

ISAAC IBN GI'AT was born in Lucena. Under his spiritual leadership and authority the city became the leading light of Jewish scholarship throughout the western Mediterranean. He was deeply attached to the family of Samuel ha-Nagid, and when the latter's son was killed in 1066, he welcomed his family who had fled from Granada into his own home. Samuel's grandson also died young, however, at the age of 20.

Isaac was a prolific writer of Talmudic and Biblical commentaries. His poetic fame rests mainly on his liturgical work, in which he displayed familiarity not only with traditional modes of thought, but also with philosophy and the physical sciences. Moses ibn Ezra was numbered among his pupils.

He died in Cordoba in 1089, and was buried in Lucena.

The Greatness of God

I know you by a name, high and renowned.
I see you in your acts but not by sight.
The secrets of your knowledge have wearied sages.
Your supreme knowing is above our state.
I search you out, and, among my thoughts,
I find you, I see you, within my own heart.
You have breathed in me a soul, linked to your throne,
Living in a body, low and contrite.
A man who is seen and cannot see, can he grasp
The glory of the unseen, seeing Great?

MOSES IBN EZRA

MOSES BEN JACOB IBN EZRA was one of four distinguished brothers from Granada. He was born not later than 1055. We have no record of what became of him during the persecution of the Jews in Granada in 1066, but it may have been at this time that he went to Lucena to study under Isaac ibn Gi'at. At all events, we find him in Granada again when the Jewish community was re-established there, and he gathered round him a circle of scholars and poets, both Jewish and non-Jewish, among whom was the young Judah ha-Levi. His early poetic achievement in Granada received great acclaim.

However, in 1090, he once again witnessed the devastation of Granada, by the Berbers, who had come to Spain a year previously from North Africa, to bolster the Muslims against the growing power of the northern Christian kingdom of Castille. The family of ibn Ezra became scattered. Moses seems to have remained in Granada for a time, impoverished and destitute, and then family dissension forced him to leave his beloved Granada for good. The details of this quarrel are not clear. But from Moses' own writings, both his brothers Judah and Isaac, and the latter's daughter, were involved. It is held by some scholars that Moses wished to marry his niece, but encountered her father's opposition. But Schirmann categorically refutes this.

Moses died between 1135 and 1140, and he spent his last years in Christian Spain, longing for the physical and intellectual environment of his birth-place. In addition to his poetical work, Moses ibn Ezra wrote a comprehensive treatise on poetry, and a philosophical work, called 'The Bed of Spices'.

The Garden of Song

All who are sick at heart and cry in bitterness,
Let not your soul complain in grief.
Enter the garden of my songs, and find balm
For your sorrow, and sing there with open-mouth.
Honey compared with them is bitter to the taste,
And before their scent, flowing myrrh is rank.
Through them the deaf hear, the stutterers speak,
The blind see, and the halting run.
The troubled and grief-stricken rejoice in them,
All who are sick at heart, and cry in bitterness.

The Coming of Spring

Winter-time has fled like a shadow;
Its storms and gales have already ceased.
And the sun, with its own circumscribed law,
Is full in the Ram, like a king at his feast.
The hills have put on their turbans of flowers,
And the plains their garments of herb and grass.
Let the earth release her scent for our nostrils,
Pent up in her folds till winter could pass.
Give me the cup to enthrone my joy,
And to relieve my heart of its pain.
And temper its heat only with tears
For its angry fire's a-flame.
Beware of Fate; for all her gifts
Are the drops of honey in vipers' tongues.
Deceive your soul with her bounty at morning,
And await her treachery when the night comes.
Drink all day long, till the light turns,
And the sun stamps the silver with its golden seal;
And all through the night, till she flies like a negress,
And the hand of the dawn takes hold of her heel.

The Sources of my Being

I wakened my thoughts from slumber
To put to sleep the desire of my heart and eyes.
And the vagaries of Fortune I perused in my mind
To attune my ears to the events to come.
And the mouth of my thought told me great things,
And placed before me the wondrous deeds of my Lord,
And told me the inaccessible mysteries,
Until I thought I was neighbour to the sons on high.
I saw in my brain a vision of the Almighty,
And I knew that within me there was God.
His magnificent splendour was hidden,
But he was revealed in deed before the eyes of thought.
In my body he has kindled a lamp from his glory;
It tells me of the paths of the wise.
It is the light which shines in the days
Of youth, and grows brighter in old age.
Were it not derived from the mystery of his light
It would fail with my strength and my years.
With it I search out the chamber of wisdom,
And I climb with no ladder to the garden of delights.

My life he has set as nothing, and I shall walk
In the way that all walked before me.
I shall journey as my fathers journeyed.
I shall rest where my forebears rested.
And in all things will God bring me to judgement.
My deeds will be both witnesses and judge.
And so I despise to dwell in the world,
To be seduced and deceived by pride.
I forsake her, before she forsakes me,

And let her take off my shoe and spit in my face.
Even if she made the sun my crown
And the moon to be my ornament
And the Great Bear a bracelet for my arm
And her young a necklace round my throat
I should not desire her strength,
Even if she housed me among the spheres of heaven.
But my desire is to fill my bowl
At the gate of instruction, and to dwell with the wise.
And how I yearn to turn their way,
But my feet are dragged by cords of iniquity
Among a people who do not know me.
I am not of them, and they are not mine.
When I speak, I give the kiss of peace,
And they believe I snap at them with my teeth.

The wisdom of the departed I regard as my portion,
And their writings are a balm to my sorrow,
And among them I hold sweet discourse,
Since they are the choicest of the faithful.
And when I swim in the sea of their wisdom
I gather pearls to embroider the days,
And in them is the delight of my eyes and heart,
And of them my jubilating lips will sing—
The light of my eyes, the song in my ears, the honey in my
        mouth,
And in my nostrils the scent of cinnamon.
And of them I shall muse, and be exalted all my days,
For in them are the sources of my being.

To Isaac, his Brother

Suddenly I met the shapes of friends I had left,
Wandering in the depths of the night.
The snare of my thoughts was laid for them;
I had spread sleep's net on my bed of lament.
How long they had wandered through the desert,
Disguised in the mantle of the dark!—and I was unaware.
They visited my bed; the night was almost gone.
I was full of the throes of pain.
They lay down by my side, until there was light
In the east, and I let loose the tresses of night.
Nothing was left of their sight
But the myrrh phial's scent in my hand.
Had I known that dreams would have shown me my loved ones
I should have lain prostrate at Vision's feet.
When dawn's fingers thrust them away, the foundation of my joy
Shuddered, and I was a broken man.
The tears rained down from my eyes.
I have split my bowels with weeping.
From the depths of my sorrow I cry, 'Injustice!'
And from the womb of my exile I sob.
Sleep has not been sweet to my eyes
Since the day I set out from the west.
I am weary of my life, of travelling the world,
Of measuring its ways in vain,
Of descending its depths and rising to the clouds'
High places, until I could say, 'I have spread out the sky like a
        curtain.'
I shone like an eagle from the tops of the mountains of prey,
And now among the beasts of the forest I go.
My legs have compassed the ends of the world

Like flashes of lightning. I have strayed from sea to sea.
One journey follows another, and I have not spied
A resting-place. I have not discovered peace.
I am scorched by day by the rays of the sun.
I widen my eyes with night's black cosmetic.
And through all the vicissitudes of time
I expose my uncovered face to heat and frost,
Until my comeliness has crumbled, and my features
Are disfigured, and I am not known.

The harvest is passed, the summer-days vanish,
The winter is complete, and I am desolate.
Months go by, years change,
And I have not reached the haven of my desire.
I am forgotten like a dead man, like a vessel in pieces,
Like a stone sunk to the bottom of the sea.
I deceive my heart by saying, 'Endure!'
And I weary it with emptiness.
I would take my own flesh in my teeth
And cry aloud, and stamp with my feet,
For my soul cannot pity itself; it has
No compassion, does not seek acquittal.
And whom should I slander? I alone am the source of my grief.
With my own right hand I am wounded.
For I took no heed of the chastisement of those who knew me,
And neglected the advice of those who loved me.
How they counselled me not to trust the treacherous
Affirmations of faith, and I would not hear!
Who will tell them how my strength has gone
And how I toil all day for vanity?
My dearest friends gave me evil for good
And laughed at me in my limping days.
How the vines I planted, the seeds of truth,
Are turned now to hostile growths!
I sowed the bread of friendship,
And briars have risen from the fields of delight.
Woe on my brothers, deceitful as a drying stream,

Who sinned against me, without my sinning.
They have made me a slave of time,
While for them I made time a perpetual bondsman.
I treated them with kindness, without hope of reward.
I destroyed myself out of love for them.
And when Fate came to make war upon me,
And I was cut down to the ground through my misdeeds,
I ran to them on feet of pride;
But when I saw their anger I was crushed.
I went to their tents with an outstretched neck,
And when I returned I was lame.
They trembled when I came upon them,
As I trembled at their lying words.
They had deceived my trust with falsehoods,
And my smeared eye could not see their design
Until they were utterly sold to folly
And I could not entreat or persuade any more.
Their violence to me has clothed them with shame,
But my stature is not lessened. It grows.

O doves, that fly like a cloud towards the west,
I adjure you by the life of love itself
To carry greetings to my distant friends,
Whose tent I have pitched in my heart.
Tell them how in grief for their absence
My heart is rent, like the rending of a kid.

And the swallow who has a nest in my ribs,
In whom my soul rejoices and takes delight—
Were it not for her life, I should not desire mine,
But for death only would be my prayer.
Through her my foot was caught in exile's net,
And I struggled like a hart in a snare.
For her sake I have entered the cauldron of affliction;
I have placed my soul in the sling of a foreign land.
Weep with her, my brother. Alas for brethren!
I am a dweller in Edom. I am swallowed up.

May God do so to me, and add in his anger
To the blows of Fortune I have suffered,
If my mouth forget your affection,
If I rid my heart of your love.
In lament for you so far away, I have coloured
My garments more black than the pupils of my eyes.
The shackles of Fortune have bound my feet. I cannot stand.
I am withheld from journeying to the place of my desire.
I trust that God may wipe out my affliction
With the water of my tears, and if I have sinned
May he be gracious, and his kindly spirit revive my soul
So that I may live again after this death of mine.

Let Man Remember

Let man remember all the days of his life
He moves at the grave's request.
He goes a little journey every day
And thinks he is at rest;
Like someone lying on board a ship
Which flies at the wind's behest.

Where are the Graves?

Where are the graves of the men who have died
On the face of the earth since the days of old?
Tombstone cluttered upon tombstone,
Sleeper sleeping upon sleeper,
In holes in the dust together they lie,
Stones of chalk with stones of ruby.

Slaves and Masters

There are graves of a primeval age
In which people sleep eternally.
No jealousy, no hatred exists there.
There is no love among neighbours, no enmity.
And when I see them, I cannot determine
Which were slaves, which had the mastery.

JUDAH HA-LEVI

THE PEAK OF SPANISH HEBREW POETRY was reached in the works of Judah ben Samuel ha-Levi. He excelled in all the media of his art, and he is generally considered to be the greatest of all post-Biblical Hebrew poets.

He was born in Tudela not later than 1075. Tudela was close to the Christian part of Spain, and it is possible that as a young boy he had some experience of life in that part of the peninsula. However, he desired to pursue his learning in southern Spain among the Jews living under Muslim rule. And so he came to Granada, where he was befriended by Moses ibn Ezra—a friendship which lasted throughout ibn Ezra's period of exile in northern Spain.

After the devastation of Granada in 1090 he appears to have gone to Lucena, and also to have visited Seville. He went to Toledo after it had become part of Alfonso's kingdom of Castille. In 1109 however there was a persecution of Jews in Castille, and ha-Levi returned to the Muslim city of Cordoba. The situation of the Jews now became extremely difficult in Spain. They suffered both economically and spiritually as a result of the Christian-Muslim conflict, and there were those who foresaw complete disaster.

Judah ha-Levi believed that the redemption of the Jews would be accomplished by their return to the Holy Land. He himself determined to go on pilgrimage and settle there. He met with opposition both to his personal departure and to his ideas. But his belief became for him a strong emotional desire, and this theme forms one of the most characteristic elements of his work, both in his poems and in his philosophical dialogue, 'The Kuzari'.

Judah ha-Levi did depart from Spain for Egypt en route to the Holy Land. We know that he landed at Alexandria and visited Cairo, appreciating the life and the civilisation of the Egyptian Jews. It is probable that he died in Egypt in 1141, although a legend would have it that he succeeded in reaching Jerusalem and was slain by a Muslim horseman at the very gates of the city.

Dialogue between Israel and God

My friend, the days of my affliction have compelled me
To dwell in the scorpion's and the viper's company,
In captivity.
Have mercy on me.

My soul despairs of the rise of the dawn,
To wait and hope morn after morn.
What can I say, O my lover, when
Edom is in my citadel, born free,
And I am subject to the Arab and the Admoni,
Who oppresses me,
Like the dregs of humanity?

My name which once stood supreme
Has become, in strangers' mouths, a mark of shame.
The Ammonite, the Moabite, and Hagar's line,
Glorify themselves in visions because of me,
Despising the word of God and Palmoni,
Enticing me
By false prophecy.

Come let us return to the gardens, my friend,
To gather there both lilies and nard.
How can the doe live with the jackals' herd?
Awake to my harp, and my bells' harmony.
Yearn for my pomegranate, my wine that is spicy.
Gazelle, flee
Back to my sanctuary.

'Be ready for the end, even if it delays;
For I have not put another nation in your place.
You have chosen me. You also are my choice.
Which other people in the north, or the south, is to me
Like my son, bound as a sacrifice, my power's primacy,
Who loves me?
Which god is like me?'

Israel's Complaint

My love, have you forgotten how you lay between my breasts?
Why have you now sold me for ever to those who enslave me?
Did I not follow you through an unsown land;
Witness Seir, Mount Paran, Sin and Sinai?
How can you share my glory among those who are not mine,
When my love was yours, and your delight was in me?
Expelled towards Seir, thrust back towards Kedar,
Tried in the furnace of Greece, subjected to Persian tyranny,
Since I shall give you my love, give of your strength to me.
There is no saviour but you; no prisoner of hope but I.

Curtains of Solomon

'Curtains of Solomon, how is it you have changed
Among the tents of Kedar, without grace or glory?'

'The peoples who lived among us before
Have left us in ruins, rubble beyond repair.
The sacred vessels are in exile and profaned.
How can you want glory from a lily among thorns?'

'Pushed out by their neighbours, sought by their Lord,
He will call all of them by name, omitting no man.
Their glory as at first shall be restored at the last.
He will kindle seven times more brightly their light that
    is obscured.'

Save my People

Your anger has enveloped me. Envelop me now with love.
Shall my sin stand between me and you for ever?
How long shall I seek your companionship in vain?
I uphold your right hand. You have enslaved me to the stranger.
You who dwell on cherubs' wings, outstretched above the ark,
Arise, look down from your dwelling. Save my people, my
        Redeemer.

The Servant of God

If only I could be the servant of God who made me,
My friends could all desert me, if he would but befriend me.

My maker, and shepherd, I, body and soul, am your creation.
You perceive all my thought; you discern my intention.
You measure my journeying, my steps, my relaxation.
If you help me, who can throw me down?
If you confine me, who but you can break my bonds?

My inner heart yearns to be near to you,
But my worldly cares drive me away from you.
My paths have strayed far from the way you pursue.
O God, help me to follow your truth. Give me instruction.
Lead me gently in judgement. Stay your conviction.

I am reluctant to perform your will, in my vigour.
And so in old age what can I hope for? Of what be sure?
O God, heal me; for with you, God, is my cure.
When old age destroys me, and my strength forgets me,
Do not forsake me, my rock, do not reject me.

Broken, despairing, I remain, fearful every minute.
Because of my mocking vanity I go naked, empty-handed.
And I am stained with my iniquity, for it is abundant.
It is sin that makes a division between you and me,
And prevents my eye from seeing the light of your glory.

Incline my heart to serve in your kingdom's service.
Cleanse my thoughts that I may know your divineness.

Do not delay your healing power in the days of my sickness.
Answer, my God. Do not chastise. Do not withhold reply.
Employ me again as your servant. Say: 'Here am I.'

Heal me, my God

Heal me, my God, and I shall be healed.
Let not your anger burn, to remove me from the earth.
My potion, my medicament, depends on you
For its weakness, or its strength, its failure or its worth.
You are the one that chooses. It is not I.
For you know what is good and what is ill.
Not on my own healing do I rely.
I look only towards your power to heal.

Singing God's Praise

All the stars of the morning sing to you,
For from you it is that they send out their light.
The sons of God glorify the mighty name,
Standing at their stations, day and night.
And the congregation of the holy re-echo them,
Hastening to your house, at dawn's first light.

My Heart is in the East

My heart is in the East, and I in the depths of the West.
My food has no taste. How can it be sweet?
How can I fulfil my pledges and my vows,
When Zion is in the power of Edom, and I in the fetters of Arabia?
It will be nothing to me to leave all the goodness of Spain.
So rich will it be to see the dust of the ruined sanctuary.

Jerusalem

Beautiful heights, joy of the world, city of a great king,
For you my soul yearns from the lands of the West.
My pity collects and is roused when I remember the past,
Your glory in exile, and your temple destroyed.
Would that I were on the wings of an eagle,
So that I could water your dust with my mingling tears.
I have sought you, although your king is away,
And snakes and scorpions oust Gilead's balm.
I shall cherish your stones and kiss them,
And your earth will be sweeter than honey to my taste.

Mount Avarim

I greet you Mount Avarim. I greet you from all sides.
On you was gathered the best of men; you received the most
      precious of graves.
If you do not know him, ask the Red Sea that was divided in two;
Or ask the bush; ask Mount Sinai, and they will reply:
'He was not a man of words, and yet he was faithful to the
      mission of God.'
I have vowed to visit you soon, if God will be my help.

Self-Exhortation to make

the Journey to Israel

Are you, at fifty, pursuing your youth,
As your days are preparing to fly away?
Do you run from the worship of God,
And yearn to serve only men?
Do you seek the crowd's company and leave
The One whom all that will may seek?
Are you slow to prepare for your journey?
Will you sell your portion for a lentil stew?
Your desire continually conceives new pleasures,
But does not your soul say to you, 'Enough!'?
Exchange your desire's counsel for that of God.
Desist from pursuing your five senses.
Please your Creator in the days that remain
To you, the days which hasten by.
Do not prevaricate before his will.
Do not confront him with magic and sorcery.
Be strong like a leopard to do his command,
Swift as a gazelle, mighty as a lion.

Let your heart remain firm in the midst of the seas,
When you see the mountains heaving and bending,
And the sailors with their hands like rags,
The masters of spells tongue-tied.
They embarked on a straight course, full of joy.
But now they are forced back, overwhelmed.
The ocean is before you as your refuge!
Your only escape are the nets of the deep!
The sails tear loose and lash,

The timbers tremble and shudder,
The grip of the wind plays on the waves,
Like bearers of sheaves to the threshing.
First they are flattened to the floor of the granary,
Then are thrown high into the stacks.
When they rise up, they are as lions.
When they break, they are like serpents.
The first are pursued by the second—
Snakes whose bite is incurable.

The mighty ship falls like a speck before God.
The mast and its banner cannot withstand,
The boat and its decks are confused,
Lower, middle and upper together.
The drawers of ropes are in torment,
Men and women full of anguish.
The sailors' spirits are deep in despair.
Bodies grow weary of their souls.
The masts' strength is of no use,
The aged's counsel does not benefit.
The masts of cedar are no more than stubble,
The fir-trees are turned to reeds,
Sand thrown into the sea is straw,
The sockets of iron are like chaff.

The people pray, each to his holy one,
And you turn to the Holy of Holies.
You recall the miracles of Red Sea and Jordan,
Inscribed as they are on every heart.
You praise the One who calms the sea's roaring,
When the waves throw up their slime.
You will tell him: 'Foul hearts are pure now!'
He will remind you of the merits of your holy forbears.
He will renew his wonders when you perform for him
Song and dance of Mahlim and Mushim.
He will return the souls to their bodies,
And the dry bones will live again.

And soon the waves will be silent,
Like flocks scattered over the earth.
And when the sun enters the ascent of the stars,
And over them presides the moon, their captain,
The night will be like a negress clothed in gold tapestry,
Like a purple garment scattered with crystals.
And the stars will be bewildered in the heart of the sea,
Like exiles driven from their own homes.
And in their own image they will make light
In the midst of the sea like flaming fires.
The water and sky will be ornaments
Pure and shining upon the night.
The sea's colour will be as heaven's,
Both—two seas bound together,
And between them my heart, a third sea,
As the waves of my praise swell once again.

The Poet is Urged

to Remain in Spain

My body is a room where a heart dwells
That is bound to the wings of an eagle. Can it conquer
A man weary of life, whose whole desire
Is to smother his cheeks in the most precious of dusts?
He trembles. His tears begin to fall.
He fears to leave Spain, to travel through the world,
To embark on board ship, to cross the desert,
By the lion's den and the leopard's mountain lair.
He rebukes his friends, and decides to go.
He leaves his home and lives in the hills.
The wolves of the forests seem to him
To be as pretty as young girls in the eyes of men.
He imagines the kites to be musicians and singers,
The roar of the lion sounds like the shepherds' pipes.
He sets his delight on the burning desire of his heart.
His streams of tears are like a river's rapids.
He will go up to the hills and down to the valleys,
To fulfil his oath, and to complete his vows.
He will strike camp and pass through the land of Egypt
To Canaan, to the most precious mountain,
While his opponents' dissuasions resound about him,
And he hears and is silent, like a man of no words.

What is the use of reply or refutation,
And why make them angry, when they are all drunkards?
They congratulate him for being in the service of kings,
Which to him is like the worship of idols.
Is it right for a pious and worthy man

To be glad that he is caught, like a bird by a child,
In the service of Philistines, Hittites, and descendants of
        Hagar,
His heart seduced by alien deities
To do their will, and forsake that of God,
To deceive the Creator and serve his creatures?
The face of the skies seems black to him,
The cup of sweetness turns bitter in his mouth.
He is weary, hard-driven, oppressed, and weak,
And yearns for Carmel and Kiryath-yearim,
To ask for forgiveness by the peaceful graves.
He yearns for the ark and tablets buried there,
Where the cherubim and the engraved stones
Lie under the earth in a hidden place.
I long to pass by them, to breathe my last by their tomb.
My eyes will see them broken, and will be a source of
        streams.
All my thoughts will be terrified at Sinai,
My eyes and heart at Mount Avarim.
How shall I not weep, and pour forth my tears,
Since from there I hope for the raising of the dead,
And there is the home of miracles, the fount of prophecy,
All reflecting the glory of the Lord of Hosts?
I shall greet its dust, and make my dwelling there,
And there I shall lament as in a cemetery.
The final goal of my thought is to rest
Among the pure by the patriarchal graves.

Go, ship, and make for the land
Which contains the Shechinah's abode.
Hasten your flight, encouraged by the hand of God.
Bind your wing to the wings of the morning breeze,
For those borne along by the wind in your sails,
For the hearts torn into a thousand pieces.

And I—I fear for the sins of my youth,
All recounted in the books of my God,

And even more for the sins of old age,
Which renew themselves as the mornings change.
There is no atonement for my rebellion,
And how shall I go through the narrow passes?
I endanger myself, if I forget my transgression,
Since my soul and my blood are in the power of sin.
Yet trust remains in him, generous of forgiveness,
Who has power and strength to release the imprisoned.
And if he judges and convicts, whether harshly or lightly,
Whether for good or ill, his judgement is exact.

The Poet Remembers his Home

My desire for the living God has constrained me
To seek out the place where my princes had their thrones;
So much so that it does not leave me time
To kiss the members of my house, my friends and
        companions.
I shall not weep for the garden I have planted
And watered, so that the flowers flourish there.
I shall not remember Judah and Azarael,
Two precious buds, the choicest of my blooms,
Nor Isaac, whom I have cherished like my own,
Produce of my sun, the finest crop of my moon.
I shall almost forget the very house of prayer,
In whose school-room I took my recreation.
I shall forget the delights of my Sabbaths,
The beauty of my festivals, my Passovers' glory.
The fame I might have had I give to others;
And I leave my praises to the stultified.
I have exchanged my bowers for the shadow of the thicket,
And the strength of my bolts for the thorn's protection.
My soul, sated with the finest of spices,
Is happy with a compound of the thistle's scent.
I no longer walk on my hands and knees,
But have set my paths in the heart of the seas,
Until I find the footstool of the feet of my God.
And there I shall pour out my thoughts and my soul.
I shall stand on the threshold of his holy mount,
And set up my doors at the gates of the skies.
By the waters of Jordan my nard shall spring up,
And I shall send out shoots by the water of Shiloach.
The Lord is mine. Can I be afraid?

The angel of his mercy carries my arms.
I shall praise his name, throughout my life,
And confess my gratitude to him for ever.

The Poet Remembers his Family during a Storm at Sea

You are the trust of my soul, the object of its fear.
To you it prostrates itself always and gives thanks.
In you I rejoice when I begin my voyage.
To you I am grateful every step of the way,
As the ship spreads out its sails,
Like the wings of a stork, to carry me;
As the deep groans and roars beneath me,
Learning from my inmost fears,
Churning the waters like a cauldron,
Making the sea into a glowing crucible;
As the ships of the Kittim come to the Philistine sea,
And the Hittites descend to their ambush;
As the sea beasts strike at the boats,
The monsters expectant for their feasting;
When horror approaches, as to a woman having her
        first child,
With a baby in the womb-mouth, and no strength in her
        to bear.
But even if I lack food and drink,
Your pleasant name will be continually in my mouth.
I shall not care for home or property,
Nor for riches, nor for any loss.
I shall forsake the child of my loins,
My only daughter, the sister of my soul.
And I shall forget her son, which splits my heart,
With only his memory to recall him to me,
Fruit of my body, child of my delight.
How can Judah ever forget Judah!

But this is nothing compared to your love,
Until I come to your gates in gratitude,
And shall dwell there, considering my heart
As a sacrifice bound upon your altar.
I shall set my grave upon your land
To remain there as my testimony.

The Western Breeze

Your breeze, Western shore, is perfumed.
The scent of nard is in its wings, and the apple.
Your origin is in the merchants' treasuries,
Surely not from the store-house of the wind.
You flutter the wings of the bird, giving him freedom;
You are like flowing myrrh straight from the phial.
How much do people long for you, since, with your help,
They are carried by wooden beams on the backs of the
        waves.
Do not let your hand slacken its hold on the ship,
Whether the day is encamped, or blows fresh at the dawn.
Smooth out the deep, split the heart of the seas,
Come to the holy mountains. There you can rest.
Rebuke the East wind which enrages the sea,
Turning the waves into a boiling cauldron.
What shall a man do, chained to his Rock,
At one time confined, at another set free.
The essence of my request is in the hand of the Highest,
Who formed the mountains, who created the wind.

Storm at Sea

I

With fainting heart and shaking knees I cry
To God. Terror invades my limbs
When the oarsmen are dumbfounded at the deep
And the sailors cannot summon up their strength.
Can I feel differently when I am suspended
On shipboard between sea and sky?
I stagger and reel. But this is easy to bear
Until I dance in your midst, O Jerusalem.

II

In the heart of the seas I shall say to my heart,
Fearful and trembling at the roar of the waves;
'If you have faith in God who made
The sea, and whose name will not fade,
Do not be frightened as the breakers rise.
He is at your side, and he has set a limit for the sea.'

The Army of Old Age

When a grey hair appeared all on its own
Upon my head, I cut it down.
'You are the victor now,' it said,
'But what will you do, once my banners are spread?'

To Moses ibn Ezra,

in Christian Spain

How, after you, can I find rest?
You go, and my heart goes with you.
Were I not to wait for the day of your return,
Then your departure would have made my death complete.
Look, the mountains of Bether testify
That the clouds are miserly, and my tears abundant.
Return to the West, lamp of the West.
Become a seal on every heart and hand.
Why do you with your pure lips linger among stammerers?
Why does the dew of Hermon appear on Gilboa?

Among the Jews of Seville

He who has been reared in scarlet
Cannot believe that his end will be the worm.
Time passes round its cup of pleasures to men
Unrecognised, but to me it is known.
They savour its taste, and proclaim it honey.
And I too partake, and say 'It makes men reel.'
They look upon their silver as the Tree of Life,
And so the Tree of Knowledge makes them turn tail.
Hear, you deaf ones—and the man who speaks
To an ear that listens is a fortunate being—
Why do you think wisdom is a burning coal?
If you only possessed it, it would be a golden ring.

But how can they hunt for it, since they prefer sleep,
Since God has made even their paragons toothless?
How can this burden be borne by dozing asses,
Who labour enough just to carry their saddles?
The herd of beasts crouch continually by the wall
And they do not know before whom they kneel.
If they swear by God, do not believe them,
Because they swear by a Being whom they do not know
        at all.
'Away!' they say to God, and refuse to know
The way to trace his paths, the secret of his law.
No one can be successful in the company of the mad,
Unless he converts to insanity before.

My soul might have perished in the misery
Of this people, braggart but corrupt,
Were it not for the presence of Meir,

117

Whose love makes my soul rejoice and exult.
I chose him as a place for seed, and I found
A harvest of love, a crop sown with affection,
His hands like the Tree of Life, the Tree of Knowledge
      on his lips,
His face, the face of the sun that does not know oblivion.
They see his few years, and then his brilliant mind.
Till now they have not seen perfection without a stain.
When they gaze upon this precious vine they say,
'Where was this found, where is this plant's home?'
If they had seen his fathers, they would have said,
'This is a virtue that has journeyed from father to son.'
Just as Aaron was worthy to wear the mitre of the priest,
So it is right for Meir to don his father's glorious crown.

The Apple

You have captured me with your charm, my lady;
You have enslaved me brutally in your prison.
From the very day that we had to part
I have found no likeness to your beauty.
I console myself with a rosy apple,
Whose scent is like the myrrh of your nose and your lips,
Its shape like your breast, and its colour
Like the hue which is seen on your cheeks.

My Love Washes her Clothes

My love washes her clothes in the water
Of my tears, and her brilliance makes them dry.
Having my two eyes, she does not need
Well-water. Her beauty contains the sun.

ABRAHAM IBN EZRA

LIKE JUDAH HA-LEVI BEFORE HIM ABRAHAM BEN MEIR IBN EZRA
was born in Tudela. His birth may be dated in 1092, and it is
possible that he met Judah ha-Levi in Southern Spain some
time before they both left that country in 1140.

Abraham ibn Ezra did not set out for Palestine, but
journeyed first to Rome. Subsequently we see him in
Lucca, Pisa, Mantua, Béziers, Narbonne, Bordeaux, Angers,
Rouen, and London. In all these places he endeavoured to
bring the culture of the Spanish Jews to those living in Italy,
France and England, and it is primarily due to him that
schools of poetry began to flourish in Italy and Provence,
which took the Spanish achievement as their model. He
died in 1067, possibly in London.

He was a master of many skills—a mathematician,
astronomer, grammarian, and philosopher, as well as a fine
expounder of the Biblical text. In contradistinction to many
contemporary Jewish thinkers he was a firm believer in
astrology. He suffered from poverty, it appears, throughout
his life, but he was able to face his ill-fortune with equa-
nimity and good humour. However, he had a sharp tongue
for his opponents. His humour and satire bring a new note
into the poetry of the Spanish school of Hebrew poets. This
must be seen, however, against the background of his
religious humility before the Creator, which is expressed in
some of his finest work. Abraham ibn Ezra left a large
number of poems, not all of which have been published.

Luckless

I

The planets and spheres in their stations
Changed their order when I first drew breath.
If I were to be a seller of lamps,
The sun would not set till after my death!

II

The stars in my heaven have ruined my life.
I cannot succeed however I strive.
If I were to be a seller of shrouds,
No one would die while I was alive!

I Have a Garment

I have a garment. It is like a sieve
With which to sift barley and wheat.
At the dead of night I spread it out like a tent
And the stars of heaven put through it their light.
From within it I see the moon and the Pleiades,
And, when it is bright, there peeps through Orion.
I get tired from counting all its holes
Which seem like the teeth of a saw in profusion.
A piece of thread, to sew up its rags,
Both warp and woof, would be superfluous.
If a fly landed on it with all his weight,
He, like an idiot, would soon grumble and curse.
My God, make good the repairs which it needs.
Make a mantle of praise from these tattered weeds.

God Supreme

God aloft in majesty,
Praised be his glory.

He created every form
Seen by us or unknown.
Thought's foundation
Was established with his name.
Who can understand him?

Those who see the good he does,
The paths through which he moves,
Can they deny his excellence?
Everything he has brought to birth
Lives to testify his worth.

A perceiver of his might,
Through his eyes, through his thought,
Through the prophets' inner sight,
Will confess him throughout his life,
For in his hand his soul is safe.

All Glory to his Name

To him who delights in music and rhyme,
I proclaim:
'All glory to his name.'

I consider. His work is good.
I sing to him who has numbered the world,
And created man from an earthen clod,
And has put a soul in his inmost core,
Pure,
Like a king in his tower.

He exists in all. From his hand comes all.
Nothing approximates him to the full.
Compared with him, all is null.
What shall I say? The world entire
Is poor.
His knowledge is far from man's power.

His might and the mystery of his skies are far.
Around his throne are his servants of fire.
His awe extends through the hosts of the air.
He has built his home on the waters above.
He moved
His lips. The heavens were clothed.

There are wonderful things in all his work.
Creation bears witness for his glory's sake.
To the prophets he revealed all that was dark.
The soul that appears to him to be dear
He will steer
In the pathway of those that fear.

How is it You have not

Given this Thought?

If, my soul, you do not know your end,
See a hint and a sign in your beginning.
Your foundation is nil, your building on the void,
Your entrance like your exit, your life like your ending.
Then why do you rest, and make vanity your nourishment?
Turn, for you are moving like a nomad's tent.
You will not be found when you are sought.
How is it you have not given this thought?

You have clung to your desire, which is really your foe.
You have not realised that your time is near.
Her wine has deceived you, her bread has seduced you,
Until all your battle-friends are beginning to tire.
Your armour-bearers now fight against you.
The requital is here for the evil you do.
Put your wine back into the vault.
How is it you have not given this thought?

You have sought for too long what you will leave behind,
But you can pursue the goodness of God if you will.
What is the purpose that you have in your mind,
When you repent but once, and sin all your fill—
Once for your Creator, many times for you alone.
How can your sin end when at your right hand
Stands Satan ready for the assault?
How is it you have not given this thought?

Fate has played with you, driven you to sin,
To build and possess; and still you want more.

All this will vanish, and on what can you lean?
Have you not taken delight for your reward?
You are a servant of the living God. Why
Have you enslaved yourself to the earth? Repent and find
What you will say before your Lord's court.
How is it you have not given this thought?

Why have you seduced me with nothing, O world!
I shall not respond any more, whether you give or take joys.
How can I rejoice on this earth or be sad?
I stay but a short time, whether Fate exalts or destroys,
Raises or deposes, gives peace or terrifies.
Whether I serve or be master, it is death that divides
All the links we have wrought.
How is it you have not given this thought?

On the Death of his Son, Isaac

Father of the child, draw near to mourn,
For God has taken away from you
Your son, your only son,
The son whom you love, Isaac.

I am the man who has seen
Destruction, whose joy has fled.
Alas, I have lost the fruit of my loins,
And it never came into my mind;
For I thought that in my old age
He would be well and strong.
But I have laboured in vain,
I have begotten a son, to dismay me.
For how can my heart be glad
At the death and departure of Isaac?

I shall lament and weep each minute,
And raise a plaintive cry,
When I remember how three years ago
He died in a foreign land;
How he journeyed from place to place,
My soul yearning after him,
Until I brought him back to my home,
While I wept night and day.
How many sorrows befell me!
These are the generations of Isaac!

My friend, take your leave of me.
If you console me, you grieve me.
Do not recall my soul's beloved,

Do not compel me to hear his name.
The small fire that was left to me
Fate has quenched. Can it harm me more?
It has overwhelmed me with eternal disaster.
It has taken the delight of my eyes.
My flesh and my heart have reached their end,
Together with the ending of Isaac.

God, in whose hand is all,
Who do your will with all your creatures,
Speak to the distressed heart of a father,
Who has feared your name from the day of his
        youth.
Rouse your spirit of consolation for him,
And enter into his divided soul.
He taught his beloved to fear you,
To walk in the way of his forbears.
You dictated, while he was still young,
The way for your servant, Isaac.

JOSEPH IBN ZABARA

JOSEPH BEN MEIR IBN ZABARA was born in Barcelona in
1140 and appears to have lived there for most of his life,
following the profession of physician.

His main work, *Sefer Sha'ashuim* ('The Book of Delights'),
is the first major Hebrew imitation of the Arabic *makam*
literature, i.e. a romantic collection of stories attached to a
main theme. His book is in rhymed prose interspersed with
short poems, and contains popular fables as well as long
dissertations on medical and anatomical details.

The date of his death is not known.

The Doctor

Fortune says to the fool: 'Become a quack.
You kill your patients and take their wealth.
You'll be better off than the angel of death,
Who for nothing deprives them of health.'

JUDAH AL-HARIZI

LIKE JOSEPH IBN ZABARA, JUDAH AL-HARIZI'S fame
depends mainly on his collection of rhymed prose narratives.
This is known as 'Tahkemoni'. He was born in Spain in the
second half of the twelfth century, and the end of that
century saw him living in Provence where he was engaged
in the work of translation from Arabic into Hebrew, in
which field he attained great eminence. He was a devoted
follower of Maimonides, began a translation of his com-
mentary to the Mishna, and completed a translation of his
great philosophical work, 'The Guide for the Perplexed',
much to the chagrin of Samuel ibn Tibbon, who had him-
self translated the work. Ibn Tibbon's translation, however,
has become the standard one.

At the beginning of the thirteenth century Judah al-Harizi
began to travel widely in the Near East, visiting Egypt,
Palestine, Syria and Iraq. Throughout his journeys he
managed to find support from many patrons.

In addition to his secular poetry, he also wrote poems
expressing religious devotion to the Holy Land, on the
pattern of those of Judah ha-Levi.

He died before 1235.

A Secret Kept

The girl brought me into the house of love.
She was as pure and perfect as Abigail.
When she took off her veil she revealed a form
That put to shame the beauty of Esther.
Her light shone in the darkness, made everything tremble.
The hills started to dance like rams.
I thought; 'Now our secrets are discovered.'
But she stretched out her hand like a woman of strength
And enveloped me with her jet-black hair.
So the day was immediately turned into night.

The Lute Sounds

The lute sounds at the young girl's breast,
Soothing the heart with its gracious tone;
Like a child weeping in his mother's arms,
While she sings and smiles at his tears.

SHEM TOB BEN PALQUERA

SHEM TOB BEN JOSEPH PALQUERA was born in northern Spain in 1225 and died after 1290. He was a follower and renowned exponent of Maimonides, and author of a number of moral and philosophical works.

His main achievement as a poet was his rhymed popular philosophical work *Ha-Mebakkesh* ('The Seeker'), which consists of a series of dialogues between the main character, and men of different professional and social classes.

If Fear is like a Rock

If fear is like a rock
Then I am a hammer.
If sorrow is a fire,
Then I am the sea.
When it comes, my heart
Increases its strength,
Like the moon that shines brighter
When the darkness falls.

TODROS BEN JUDAH ABULAFIA

TODROS BEN JUDAH HALEVI ABULAFIA was born in Toledo
in 1247. Alfonso of Castille attracted many Jews to his
court, and Todros was among those who sought wealthy
patrons in an effort to reach the royal favour, and he did
indeed succeed in being received by the king, to whom he
dedicated a number of verses.

One of his patrons, Don Isaac de la Maleha, was executed
by the king in 1279, and Todros himself was imprisoned
with many other Jews of Castille, and held for ransom. In
1281, however, he was released amid circumstances un-
known to us. He appears to have received the approbation of
Alfonso's successor, Sancho IV.

He died not earlier than 1298.

From Prison

I

If my imprisonment has no end,
I shall receive all from God as a mark of love.
If my oppressors take all my wealth,
My heart and my mind will not be enslaved.
And if they afflict me on this earth,
My soul will rejoice in the world to come.
If they kill me, I shall sing with love
As I make my way to the house of my God.
I am glad to suffer the pain he sends,
For the reason for all comes from God.

II

Let the dew of your mercies drop upon me,
For look, my father, my leaves have fallen.
Re-establish my paths, and be with me,
For all my limbs are shaking with fear.
My enemies are many. Save me from them.
Let your love be spread over me.
See how the vultures of Fortune prey
On me, and eat my flesh all day.
Save my swallows from their depredations.
Have pity on my song-birds, on my doves.

Notes

I MAKE NO CLAIM to originality in these notes. I have simply attempted to use the resources at my disposal to clarify some points in the poems for the English reader. However, I am of course responsible for any errors.

I have used the following abbreviations:

S = the anthology by Hayyim Schirmann, *Ha-Shirah ha-Ivrith bi-Sefarad u-bi-Provence,* Jerusalem, Tel-Aviv 1954.

B = Brody and Wiener's anthology, *Mibchar ha-Shirah ha-Ivrith,* Leipzig 1922.

Singer = *Authorised Daily Prayer Book,* translated by S. Singer, London. New edition 1962.

Quotations from the Bible are taken mainly from the translation published by the Jewish Publication Society of America.

DUNASH HA-LEVI BEN LABRAT

page 15 *Reply to an Invitation to a Feast* S. I,34.

This poem represents the spiritual dilemma of the Jew under Muslim rule in time of peace. On the one hand, he is tempted to submit to the influence of his environment, to the neglect of his national and religious heritage; on the other, he is oppressed by the condition of exile imposed upon him.

And pleasant anemones. Cf. Is. 17, 10, where the usual translation is 'plants of pleasantness'. But see Brown, Driver and Briggs, *Hebrew Lexicon* s.v. *na'aman.* Ibn Ezra, commenting on this phrase, also refers to an Arabic name, without however specifying a particular flower.

As if thinking of music. The verb used (*hagah*) is the same as that trans-

147

lated as 'moaning' in the previous line. Hebrew poets often used the identical word twice in close conjunction, with a differentiation in meaning. In medieval times the verb was often used in the sense of 'meditate' or 'think'.

Ease our weary bones. More literally, 'put sorrows to flight'.

I shall go out to the herd. The use of the personal pronoun, as here, is unusual in Hebrew usage, and generally indicates emphasis. Whereas, in this case, our poet may have used it for metrical reasons, it is also possible that he alludes to the act of Abraham in Gen. 18, 7, who himself ran to the herd to select an animal for his guests, a gesture of hospitality for which he received much praise from Rabbinic commentators.

You scorn the Divine. More literally, 'like scorners and fools'.

page 17 *A Song for the Sabbath* S. I, 40.

He will proclaim freedom. The subject is God. The Sabbath is connected with freedom. The commandment to observe the Sabbath (Deut. 5, 15) connects it expressly with the exodus from Egypt. The *Kiddush* on Friday evening proclaims that the Sabbath is a memorial of the creation, and a remembrance of the Exodus.

And will keep you. That is, Israel.

my portals and my home. The poet now addresses God directly, speaking in the name of Israel. The phrase refers to the ruins of the Temple and Jerusalem.

Plant a vine in my vineyard. See Is. 5, 2ff, and Jer. 2, 21. The poet asks that Israel be given a new lease of life in its homeland, now that Israel has received punishment for its sins.

Tread the wine-press in Bozrah. See Is. 63, 1ff. Bozrah was a city of Edom, and Edom was a symbol of the power of Rome, and later of Christianity.

And in Babylon. Among Arabic-speaking Jews, Babylon was a symbol of Baghdad, centre of the Muslim Empire (Schirmann).

Give those who teach and those who obey. The poet refers to the custodians of Jewish law and those who follow their teachings.

like the flow of a stream. Schirmann compares Is. 66, 12, 'For thus saith the Lord, Behold, I will extend peace to her like a river.'

for your power. Added.

know wisdom. The poet, once more, addresses Israel. Wisdom is identified with Torah, which enjoins the observance of the Sabbath.

page 21 *Sanctification* B, 58.

This poem was to be recited in conjunction with that part of the morning liturgy of the Day of Atonement which describes the praising of God by the angels. The Jewish conception of angelic beings has its starting-point in the first chapter of Ezekiel. The creatures (*hayyoth*) and the wheels (*ofannim*) of that chapter are taken to represent different classes of angels. According to one Rabbinic concept the angels do not begin to praise God in heaven until Israel has begun to praise him on earth. (For this and other relevant material see Hullin 91b.) This is at the root of the division in our poem.

For the relevant liturgy of the normal morning service see Singer pp. 39f. and 47, and compare Is. 6, 1-3; and Ezekiel 3, 12.

In the heights of heaven is the throne of your dwelling, And among the earthbound is your dominion's strength. Compare the Targum to Isaiah 6, 3: 'Holy in the exalted heavens above, the house of his dwelling; holy upon the earth, the work of his power.'

These . . . these. i.e. those in heaven, and those on earth.

five prayers. The five services of the Day of Atonement viz. Evening, Morning, Additional, Afternoon, and Concluding.

where? 'Where is the place of God's glory?'

Possessors of the engraved law. The written law believed to have been transmitted unchanged since Moses received it on Sinai.

page 23 *A Song for the New Year* S. I, 56.

This poem is rhymed in the original but not metrical. Each stanza ends with a biblical quotation, viz. Psalm 65, 2; Job 38, 5; Lamentations 3, 37; Proverbs 30, 4; Job 38, 25; 21, 31; 9, 4; Proverbs 30, 4.

The world was considered by one Rabbinic tradition to have been created in Tishri, on the first of which month occurs the Jewish New Year. Hence this song of praise for God the Creator. The poem is based largely, in style and content, on Job, Chapters 38 to 41.

whose ways are humility? God's humility is apparent in two ways, according to Rabbinic teaching; firstly, in that he was modest enough to take the advice of his angels before creating man (deduced from Gen. 1, 26: 'Let us make man'), and, secondly, in that he chose the lowliest of plants, a bush, as a medium for his first revelation to Moses (Exodus 3).

Who spaces each wave at three hundred leagues? From Baba Bathra 73a:

'Rabbah said: Sailors told me that there is a distance of three hundred parasangs between one wave and another, and the height of the wave is three hundred parasangs. Once we were on a voyage and the wave lifted us up so high that we were able to see the resting-place of the smallest star.'

Who brings each drop from its own mould to promote fertility? An interpretation of Job 38, 25 runs: 'I have created many rain-drops in the clouds, and for each rain-drop I have created a special mould so that two rain-drops should not come from the same mould, for if two raindrops were to come from the same mould, they would wash away the soil and it would not bear crops.' (*Baba Bathra* 16a). See Ginzberg, 'The Legends of the Jews' II, 227 and V, 383. Our verse reads literally, 'who prevents two drops coming from the same mould and washing (the soil) away?'

the ninety-nine groans of the mountain goat. i.e. when she bears her young. In *Tanhuma Emor*, 11 we find, 'Of the hundred cries which a woman emits when she is about to give birth . . . ninety-nine are for death, and one is for life.' The following verse is based on *Baba Bathra* 16af. 'The mountain-goat is cruel to her young. When she is about to give birth, she climbs up to the topmost crag, so that her young should fall from it and die. But I summon an eagle to catch it in her wings and place it before its mother, and if the eagle were one second too soon or too late, it would be killed.' See Ginzberg, loc. cit.

Who supplies the snake to bite the hinds as they bear? lit. 'bite the wombs of the hinds'. *Baba Bathra* 16b reads: 'The womb of the hind is narrow. When she is about to give birth I summon a serpent to bite the mouth of her womb, and she is delivered of her offspring. And were it to come one second too soon or too late, she would die.' See Ginzberg, loc. cit.

so his life is untrammeled. 'Many hairs have I created in man, and for each hair I have created a special sac, so that two hairs should not draw nourishment from one sac, for if two should be nourished from one sac they would impair the sight of man.' (*Baba Bathra* 16a).

five terrors. 'There are five fears, and they are the fear that the strong have for the weak: the lion's fear of the Ethiopian fly, the elephant's fear of the gnat, the scorpion's fear of the spider, the eagle's fear of the swallow, the leviathan's fear of the stickleback.' (*Shabbat* 77b). For the last see Ginzberg, op. cit. I, 27 and V, 42.

the hidden leviathan. According to Rabbinic tradition, leviathan is now concealed from our sight, but will be revealed to the righteous in the world to come.

page 25 *Lament on the Devastation of the Land of Israel* (1012) S. I, 64.

The title refers to the persecution in Israel which took place during the Caliphate of Hakim of Egypt, who has been called 'The Mahometan Caligula', and who attempted to convert forcibly both Jews and Christians to Islam.

Like the lament of Hadadrimmon . . . See Zechariah 12, 11 and 2 Kings 23, 29.

barbarians. lit. Cushites, a term used for the Africans of what is now the Sudan, and Ethiopia.

of pregnant women. lit. of ripped pregnant women.

sculptured marble. lit. from Psalm 144, 12, 'Whose daughters are as corner-pillars carved (after the fashion of a palace)'.

Forced to be slaves to the ignoble. lit. servants of servants. This refers to the ancestry of the Muslims which is traced back to Ishmael, son of Hagar, Sarah's Egyptian servant, (Genesis 16).

forlorn. Added.

Weep for those . . . I have slightly expanded this verse.

ISAAC IBN KALPON

page 29 *A Present of Cheese* S. I, 70.

As Elkanah remembered Peninah. Referring to 1 Samuel 1, 4: 'Elkanah . . . gave to Peninah his wife, and to all her sons and her daughters, portions.'

SAMUEL HA-NAGID

page 33 *In Praise of Wine* S. I, 163.

. . . whose blood is mixed with his tears. That acute grief provoked tears of blood mingled with water was a common conceit among medieval Hebrew poets.

page 34 *An Invitation* S. I, 165.

Come out and see the morning light. The imperative here is in the plural. It was not unusual to hold wine-feasts at dawn.

My soul Revives and then dies. The songs awaken desire in his heart, but he 'dies' when he finds his love unreciprocated (Schirmann).

page 35 *The Power of the Pen* S. I, 141.

His pen can raise a man to the rank. Good penmanship and a fine literary style were essential prerequisites for preferment at court. The poet's own life provides evidence of this.

page 36 *On the Death of his Brother.*
The following three poems are taken from a cycle of elegies which Samuel ha-Nagid wrote on the death of his older brother, Isaac, in 1041. I. S. I, 107; B. 71.

... *one day ago.* Schirmann notes that the Arabic inscription to this poem relates that the poet visited his brother's grave on the morrow of the funeral. It should be noted that according to Jewish practice it is not customary for the mourner to leave his house during the first seven days of mourning which begin immediately after the burial. Similarly, the line *I bear you greetings* gains a certain poignancy when one realises that it is forbidden for a mourner to proffer a greeting during the first seven days of mourning.
II. B. 72.

The days of my mourning. i.e. the first seven days.

... *in my majesty and high estate.* See the biographical introduction.

page 37.
III. S. I, 108; B. 72.

face ... like. The same Hebrew word is used here.

when I too change. i.e. until I die. The phrase is found in Job 14, 14, upon which verse see the comment of Abraham ibn Ezra.

page 39 *Man Runs towards the Grave* S. I, 135.

in the heart of the tomb. lit. in the heart of Sheol.

page 40 *The Old Man's Warning* S. I, 135.

page 41 *The Hour in which I am* S. I, 131.

page 42 *Two Bouts of Woe* S. I, 130.

page 43 *I Look up to the Sky* S. I, 136.

like a tent Constructed with loops and hooks. This simile is taken from Exodus, Chapter 26, which describes the construction of the tabernacle in the wilderness.

Sending her sheep into the reeds. A curious image. One would not expect sheep to feed very happily among reeds. The poet relies on

Gen. 41, 2, where reeds are considered to be fit pasture for cattle.

page 44 *The Citadel* S. I, 132.
. . . *the builders and destroyers* . . In this and following verses I have occasionally altered the order of the Hebrew.
womb. lit. heart.

page 45 *God's Assurance* S. I, 78.
See Isaiah 43, 2: 'When thou passest through the waters, I will be with thee, and through the rivers, they shall not overflow thee; When thou walkest through the fire, thou shalt not be burned, Neither shall the flame kindle upon thee.'
in your help. lit. in your salvation, and your uplifting.
Michael . . . Gabriel. Both angels in Rabbinic tradition were guardians of individual Jews, and of the Jewish people generally. Gabriel, especially, was considered to be an angel of fire and of war. However, no precise agreed delimitation was fixed for their respective duties. For further information, see Ginzberg, Legends, Index volume, s.v. Gabriel and Michael, and especially V. 70f. where Michael and Gabriel are compared.
your chariot. i.e. God's glorious throne and his retinue, the image of which is taken from Ezekiel 1. The Hebrew of this line is obscure. Perhaps we should translate 'your chariot, which is above me, and all that surrounds you,' or 'your chariot, which protects me, and all that surrounds you.'

page 46 *The Victory over Ben Abbad* S. I, 94; B. 65.
At the head of this poem there is an Arabic inscription which reads as follows: The victory over the men of Abbad came at the approach of evening on that day (i.e. on the 13th of Tishri 1039), and Ben Abbad was killed as dusk fell on the Friday evening, at the eve of the Feast of Tabernacles, and the Prince said this song, and called it 'A Song of Praise' (Schirmann).
It describes the victory of the forces of Badis, king of Granada, who were commanded by the poet, over the army of Seville, under the command of Ismail ibn Abbad. The first half of the eleventh century saw the rise of no less than twenty states under their own petty kings. Quarrels frequently broke out among them. These preceded the re-conquest of Spain by the growing Christian power in the North.
Shall I every year pass through . . . Compare the imagery of this and the following lines with that of the preceding poem, 'God's Assurance'.

the cowards. lit. those who turn back. The verb *sug* is used here in order to pun with *sig,* 'dross'.

those who wear fringes. i.e. the Jews who wear fringed garments in order to comply with the Biblical commandment in Numbers 15, 38f.

Ben Abbas. Samuel had defeated him the previous year at Alfuente during the conflict between Badis, king of Granada, and Zuhair of Almeria. Samuel wrote a poem about this battle also. In it Zuhair is called Agag; his people, the Salabim, Amalekites; and Ben Abbas, Haman. Ben Abbas had earlier attempted to persuade Badis to dismiss Samuel from his court.

Ben Abbad. The commander of the forces of Seville.

the crown of majesty. Ismail ibn Abbad was the son of the ruler of Seville, whereas Ben Abbas had not been of royal lineage.

of the Berbers. lit. of Philistia (Schirmann).

my king. Badis of Granada.

Then he set out. i.e. Ben Abbad.

a city and a kingdom. This refers to his depredations in the area of Carmona (Schirmann).

making The children of the living God suffer their reproaches. lit. the children of the living God were stoned with the stones of their tongues.

and brought shackles for their feet. Ps. 60, 10 is interpreted by some Rabbinic authorities as 'I shall cast my shackles against Edom.' Or, we may translate 'took the shoes from their very feet'. This rendering would refer to the symbolic act which accompanied purchase, thus meaning that the Jews were enslaved. Cf. Ruth 4, 7f., and Ps. 60, 10 (= 108, 10). See the later verse of this poem, 'All those who took for pledges The shoes and garments of God's people.'

Nor by flabbiness on their loins. See Lev. 3, 4 etc. 'and the two kidneys, and the fat that is on them, which is by the loins,' of a sacrificial animal.

red as rolled parchment. Parchment made of deer-skin is red, and is commonly found in Mediterranean lands. In the Jewish Museum in London there is a Torah scroll from North Africa made of red parchment.

brow-plates. This Hebrew term occurs in the Bible only in the description of the armour of Goliath (I Sam. 17, 6) where it is usually translated 'greaves'. But the word is connected with the Hebrew for 'brow'. (See Rashi and Kimchi ad. loc.) Here it probably refers to a long narrow metal protection which would project from the helmet between the eyes. Schirmann wonders whether it might be leg-armour.

the glint. Brody's text has *lahem* (to them) for *lahat* (glint).

And he left in haste ... This and the three following lines are not found in Brody's text.

on the bank of the river. i.e. the River Jenil (Schirmann).

as at the battle of the ravine. Numbers 21, 15 'the slope of the valleys'. The phrase occurs in a quotation from the 'Wars of the Lord' (v. 14). Rashi describes it as the scene of a battle with the Amorites.

dead Agag. i.e. Zuhair. See above.

their male warriors. lit. husbands.

force of Amalek. i.e. the Salabim. See above.

And princes refusing to take up the fight. A general of Malaga, an ally of Granada, fled with his army at the beginning of the battle (Schirmann).

his seventy armies. lit. seventy banners. The throne of God was surrounded by seventy angels, according to Rabbinic tradition, to each of which one of the seventy nations of the world was assigned.

from the dust. The patriarchs, Abraham, Isaac, and Jacob, because of their great merit, are able to intercede before God from their graves, on behalf of the Jews.

the sons of the giants. lit. the Nephilim. Cf. Numbers 13, 33: 'And there we saw the Nephilim, the sons of Anak, who come of the Nephilim; and we were in our own sight as grasshoppers, and so we were in their sight.'

went out. To battle.

not by a window. Compare Cant. 2, 9: 'Behold, he standeth behind our wall, He looketh in through the windows.' According to Rabbinic interpretation of the 'Song of Songs', this represents God, ready to protect his afflicted people. Samuel emphasises that God is not only prepared, but, in this case, acts openly to save his people.

that had not yet touched ground. Because of a life of luxury (Schirmann).

For an abode in the wild woods. Reading with Brody.

ve-ya'ar. Schirmann's text has *ve-yachad* (together).

useless gravel. The Hebrew term *pesulim* means 'unfit for use', and here it has the overtone of 'carved'. (An idol is *pesel*). One might translate, therefore, 'their arrows were shaped like gravel'.

On the second day. The battle began on the second day, and the rout of the enemy was on the fifth day (Schirmann).

the Berber. lit. Philistia. See above.

the son of Abraham. lit. the son of Ethan. See Ps. 89, 1. Ethan the Ezrahite is identified with Abraham in Baba Bathra 15a, and this Psalm is attributed to him. There is an allusion here to the salvation of Isaac on

Mount Moriah, which took place on the first of Tishri, according to Rabbinic tradition.

in the month Of the flowing rivers. Hebrew *Ethanim.* See Rosh Hashanah 11a: 'Whence do we know that the patriarchs were born in Tishri? Because it says: 'And all the men of Israel assembled themselves unto King Solomon at the feast, in the month *Ethanim,* which is the seventh month' (1 Kings 8, 2). That is the month in which the mighty ones (*Ethanim*) were born.'

And after the departure of the ninety-ninth year. The victory took place at the beginning of the year 4800 according to the Jewish calendar. The Jewish New Year begins in Tishri, 'the seventh month'.

the profane. lit. uncircumcised. This is clearly not to be taken literally, since the Muslims do circumcise.

drops from a storm-cloud. The Hebrew *'agalim* occurs only in Job 38, 28, where it refers to dewdrops. This meaning is hardly suitable here. See *Hagigah* 12b where there is reference to a store of *'agalim:* 'There are (in Heaven) stores of snow, and stores of hail, and the loft of harmful dews, and the loft of raindrops (*'agalim*), the chamber of the whirlwind and storm, and the cave of vapour . . .'

the eve of Gathering. A name for the festival of Succoth, or Tabernacles, which begins on the eve of the fifteenth of Tishri.

the night of Abram. See Gen. 14, 15, which deals with Abram's victory over the five kings.

the night of Moses. See Exodus 11, 4—the slaying of the Egyptian first-born.

Joshua's noon-day. See Joshua 10, 12ff.—Joshua's victory over the Amorites when 'the sun stood still'.

the night when the siege was raised. See 2 Kings 19, 35ff.—the sudden raising of the siege of Jerusalem by Sennacherib. The Hebrew means literally 'the removal of burdens' (Schirmann's text) or 'the bearing of burdens' (Brody's text). The episode referred to may be the Exodus from Egypt. At all events, all the victories mentioned are directly or indirectly attributed by the Rabbis to God's intervention.

the dwellers in tents. i.e. the descendants of Jacob. See Genesis 25, 27.

Shofar-day. i.e. *Rosh ha-Shanah,* the New Year, when the ram's horn (*shofar*) is sounded.

Yom Kippur. The Day of Atonement.

the pilgrims' feasts. The three festivals on which it was obligatory in Temple times to make a pilgrimage to Jerusalem. They were Tabernacles, Passover, and the Feast of Weeks.

some less rigorous. Even though some maintain that it is permitted to break the law at a time of danger (Schirmann).

when work was forbidden. On Sabbaths and festivals. The battle was fought and won between the Sabbath and the coming of Succoth.

Myrtle from the hills . . . The Jews bring four 'kinds' of vegetation to their 'tabernacles' at Succoth viz., palm, willow, myrtle, and citron. In the lines that follow there are constant puns on these words.

the half-shekel. See Exodus 30, 11-16.

by the waters. The River Jenil. See above.

psalms of praise. i.e. the *Hallel*, Psalms 113-118, recited on festivals.

What am I, what is my life? Compare the prayer in the morning liturgy (Singer p. 9), translated partially in the Introduction, page 2.

To him I have already composed a song. This refers to the poem he composed to celebrate his victory over Ben Abbas a year earlier.

the psalmist's praises. Each poem, in the original, consists of 149 lines. Our present book of Psalms has 150 psalms. But according to an ancient enumeration 149 were counted.

And when, in the future, your sons ask. Cf. Exodus 13, 14: 'And it shall be when thy son asketh thee in time to come, saying: "What is this?" that thou shalt say unto him . . .'

you will reply. lit. those asked will reply.

page 55 *A Message to his Son, Joseph, on the Raising of the Siege of Lorca* S. I, 117; B. 70.

In 1042 the forces of Granada raised the siege of Lorca, which was under attack from a coalition of eastern Spanish princes. The poet has also left a poem, addressed to his son, which describes his great apprehension as to the outcome of the battle.

sweetened with saffron-water. It was customary to add perfume to a letter.

to Joseph's house. In Granada (Schirmann).

falling upon each other. Because of their intense panic.

like thieves. lit. like a thief.

like the skin to one's face. lit. 'as the lobe is attached to the liver', an image taken from Exodus 29,13.

when I was in trouble. lit. 'when it (my soul) was in trouble'.

a pen of iron. lit. 'a pen of iron and lead'.

page 57 *War* S. I, 142.

page 58 *Israel Arise* S. I, 146.

wicked queen. Apparently this refers to the kingdom of Edom, symbolising Christianity. See Berachoth 61b.

Gazelle of Senir. An image taken from the Song of Songs, which is regarded by the Rabbis as a dialogue between God and Israel. See Cant. 4, 8: 'Come with me from Lebanon, my bride, With me from Lebanon; Look from the top of Amana, From the top of Senir and Hermon.'

Raise yourself. I have reversed the order of the last two lines.

page 59 *The Wounded Lion* S I, 139.

SOLOMON IBN GABIROL

page 63 *An Apple for Isaac* S. I, 220.

page 64 *The Writing of Winter* S. I, 219.

of violet and purple. A description of the flowers that emerge as a result of the winter-rains.

No human being. lit. such things are not in the power of the thinker in his thoughts. Cf. I Sam. 2, 3 where the *Ketiv* is interpreted by David Kimchi as 'the actions of men cannot be established unless God wills it.'

page 65 *In Mourning for Yekutiel* S. I, 202.

Yekutiel ben Isaac ibn Has'an was a wealthy and learned patron of Solomon. He was imprisoned and executed, for reasons that are unknown to us, in 1039.

page 66 *On the Death of Rab Hai* S. I, 203.

Rab Hai, the last of the great Babylonian Gaonim, died at the academic centre of Pumbeditha in 1039.

the ark which now lies hidden in Zion. The ark of the covenant, according to Rabbinic tradition, lies buried within the Temple precincts in Jerusalem.

page 67 *Separation from the Torah* S. I, 194.

to hear the Sefer Torah. The poet was too ill to go to the synagogue to hear the prescribed reading from the Scroll of the Law.

page 68 *His Illness* S. I, 194.

And do not look at . . . lit. do not punish the sin of dust and earth. However, the Hebrew verb *faqad* has the basic meaning of 'look to, attend'. The Authorised translation is 'visit the iniquity'.

the decree. i.e. the decision of God that the poet should die.

consider my illness as my redemption. i.e. let the pain that I suffer be sufficient punishment and atonement for my sin, and let me not die.

page 69 *In the Morning I Look for you* S. I, 238; B. 78.

This poem was written to be said in conjunction with the *Nishmath* prayer ('The soul of every living being shall bless thy name, O Lord our God'—Singer p. 173). The prayer forms part of the morning liturgy for Sabbaths and Festivals.

page 70 *The Unity of God* S. I, 249.

Thirty-two paths make up your way. See *Sefer Yetsirah* I, 1. Cf. Scholem, 'Major Trends in Jewish Mysticism' page 76. He says of the *Sefer Yetsirah*, 'Its chief subject-matters are the elements of the world, which are sought in the ten elementary and primordial numbers— *Sefiroth* as the book calls them—and the twenty-two letters of the Hebrew alphabet. These together represent the mysterious forces whose convergence has produced the various combinations observable throughout the whole of creation; they are the "thirty-two secret paths of wisdom" through which God has created all that exists.'

All that perceive them. lit. all who understand their mystery (i.e. the mystery of the paths).

ISAAC IBN GI'AT

page 73 *The Greatness of God* S. I, 304.

a name, high and renowned. Or 'the name "High" and "Renowned" '.

in your acts, but not by sight. God is not physical; so he cannot be apprehended by the senses. But he is manifested in his creation.

Your supreme knowing is above our state. Schirmann interprets this verse differently: 'The knowledge of matters which are beyond the grasp of the intellect is not given to us, and the pursuit of them only brings weariness.'

linked to your throne. There is a Rabbinic tradition that God created the souls of all men at the time of the creation of the world, and he has, as it were, a store of them by him, ready to be despatched into the world. See Ginzberg, op. cit. I, 56 and V, 75.

who is seen and cannot see. Man is seen by God, but cannot see God.

MOSES IBN EZRA

page 77 *The Garden of Song. Shire ha-Chol* (ed. Brody). Berlin 1935, Vol I page 3. This poem prefaces the collection of the poet's secular work in the above-named edition.

Before their scent. This not only carries on the imagery of the garden, but is also to be taken literally. Writers would perfume their letters, and mix spices with their ink.

page 78 *The Coming of Spring* S. I, 372; B. 146.

Its storms and gales. lit. 'its horsemen and its chariot' meaning 'its retinue'. Cf. 2 Kings 2, 12, where Elisha cries after the ascent of Elijah 'My father, my father, the chariots of Israel and the horsemen thereof.'

Is full in the Ram. The sun has entered the zodiacal house of the Ram.

to enthrone. Hebrew *yasir.* lit. 'to make a prince of'. The text in Brody's edition reads *yashiv* ('to restore').

temper its heat. This refers to the mixing of wine with water.

drops of honey in vipers' tongues. lit. 'like the poison of the viper which contains a little honey'. This belief was prevalent in medieval times.

till she flies like a negress. The original uses the masculine form.

page 79 *The Sources of my Being* S.I, 399; B. 147.

His magnificent splendour was hidden. This is Brody's text. Schirmann reads 'the glory of his essence'.

But he was revealed in deed. Compare the poem of Isaac ibn Gi'at on page 73 and the note thereon.

he has kindled a lamp from his glory. i.e. my soul derives from God. Cf. Proverbs 20, 27: 'The spirit of man is the lamp of the Lord.' According to the punctuation in Schirmann's text 'from his glory' belongs to the following verse. Brody has 'and my glory tells me . . .'

grows brighter in old age. Because of the growth in intellectual power, which according to medieval Jewish philosophers, was related to, or, in the view of some, identical with, the soul. Alternatively, the verse may mean that the soul grows brighter as it gets nearer to its original home.

Were it not derived. Were the soul not derived from the spirit of God, it would deteriorate in conjunction with the physical being.

the garden of delights. 'The world of the souls which is beneath the throne of glory' (Schirmann). Compare the phrase 'linked to your throne' in the poem by Isaac ibn Gi'at above, and the note thereon. 'The garden of delights' would refer also to the pleasures of the intellect.

both witnesses and judge. They will attest my conduct, and they themselves will therefore produce the judgment.

And let her take off my shoe and spit in my face. This describes the ceremony of *Halitsah* (Deut. 25, 9)—an act performed by a childless widow with her deceased husband's brother who has refused to enter into levirate marriage with her. After this act the widow was free to marry whomever she chose. It denotes here the complete severance between the world and the poet.

Even if she housed me among the spheres of heaven. Brody's text has *'atunay* for *me'onay* i.e. 'even were she to make my garments of the heavenly spheres', a beautiful image, but perhaps not what the poet intended.

Among a people who do not know me. The poem appears to have been written during the poet's exile. See the Biographical Introduction.

to embroider the days. lit. 'to deck the throat of the days' (Brody's text has 'to deck my throat'). Intellectual delights beautify one's otherwise prosaic existence.

page 81 *To Isaac, his Brother* B. 140.

For the background to this poem see the Biographical Introduction.

friends I had left. i.e. when the poet left his native town.

by my side. lit. 'between my breasts'.

The tears . . . lit. 'drops of the blood of my eyes'. See the note on page 151.

My bowels. lit. 'The rock of my liver'. Cf. Lamentations 2, 11. After this verse I have omitted a line which translated literally reads: 'Were it not that grief had shut me in (and prevented me from weeping) I should have drowned, I think, in a pool of tears.'

the mountains . . . the forest. The poet contrasts the brilliant company which he enjoyed in his native town with the unlettered society in which he is now compelled to live.

I would take my own flesh in my teeth. Cf. Job 13, 14.

my soul cannot pity itself. i.e. I can blame no one but myself. Otherwise I would complain to the world.

treacherous Affirmations of faith. from his brother Judah. He is referred to, for stylistic reasons, in the plural.

161

I made time a perpetual bondsman. lit. 'I pierced the lobe of the ear of time,'—an allusion to the legislation in Exodus 21, 6.

I was lame. lit. 'I stepped with a swollen foot.'

towards the west. i.e. towards Andalusia.

to my distant friends. i.e. to his brother Isaac.

like the rending of a kid. A reference to the feat of Samson in Judges 14, 6: 'he rent him (the lion) as one would have rent a kid.'

the swallow. i.e. Isaac's daughter.

Edom. i.e. Christian lands.

page 85 *Let Man Remember* S. I, 401; B. 148.

He moves at the grave's request. lit. 'he is being taken towards death.' Cf. Proverbs 24, 11: 'Deliver them that are drawn unto death.'

page 86 *Where are the Graves?* B. 148.

Tombstone cluttered upon tombstone. lit. 'one grave hewn out above another.'

page 87 *Slaves and Masters* S. I, 403; B. 150.

JUDAH HA-LEVI

page 91 *Dialogue between Israel and God* S. I, 482.

The first four verses contain the complaint and supplication of Israel; the fifth verse is God's reply.

Edom is in my citadel. Edom was a term used for the Christian nations, who were at this time in possession of Jerusalem, the Jews' 'citadel'. See Dunash ha-Levi ben Labrat, 'A Song for the Sabbath', and the notes thereon.

the Admoni. lit. 'ruddy', a description of the baby Esau in Genesis 25, 25. Esau was the ancestor of Edom. This, too, therefore, refers to the Christians.

Like the dregs of humanity. lit. 'the dogs of my flock', a derogatory phrase in Job 30, 1.

Hagar's line. The Muslims, descended from Ishmael, the son of Abraham and Hagar.

in visions. i.e. the prophetic visions of other faiths contain denunciations of the Jews.

Palmoni. lit. 'that certain one', mentioned in Daniel 8, 13, who gives the date of the redemption of Israel.

Enticing me by false prophecy. i.e. the other nations try to persuade Israel to abandon their faith.

Come, let us return. An exhortation to return to Israel, based largely on the phraseology of the Song of Songs, which is itself interpreted as a dialogue between God and Israel.

my son, bound as a sacrifice. The reference is to Isaac.

my power's primacy. A Biblical phrase, denoting the first-born son.

page 93 *Israel's Complaint* S. I, 466; B. 169.

This poem was written to be said in conjunction with the *Nishmath* prayer. See note on page 159.

My love. Israel speaks to God in the phraseology of the Song of Songs (1, 13).

Witness Seir, Mount Paran, Sin and Sinai. Places in which God manifested himself to the Israelites during their journey from Egypt to Canaan. Cf. Exodus 16, 1; Deuteronomy 33, 2.

How can you . . . I have interchanged this, and the following line.

Seir. A land of Edom. Hence, a reference to the Christian nations. See note on previous poem.

Kedar. A tribe named after the son of Ishamel (Gen. 25, 13). Hence, a reference to the Muslim nations.

Since I shall give you . . . I have interchanged this and the following line.

page 94 *Curtains of Solomon* S. I, 481; B. 158.

Curtains of Solomon . . . tents of Kedar Cf. Cant. 1, 5. Here the reference is to the Jews dwelling among the Muslims.

The sacred vessels. i.e. the utensils which formerly were used in the Temple in Jerusalem.

seven times more brightly. Cf. Isaiah 30, 26: 'Moreover the light of the moon shall be as the light of the sun, And the light of the sun shall be sevenfold, as the light of the seven days, In the day that the Lord bindeth up the bruise of His people, And healeth the stroke of their wound.'

page 95 *Save my People* S. I, 464; B. 169.

outstretched above the ark. See Exodus 25, 19ff. See also the note on the poem 'The Poet is Urged to Remain in Spain' on page 166. On God dwelling between the cherubim, see 1 Sam. 4, 4: 'The Lord of Hosts, who sitteth upon the cherubim.'

I uphold your right hand. I have translated *kannah* as 'pillar' (lit. 'I am the pillar of your right hand'). However, the phrase comes from Psalm 80, 16 where it is usually translated as 'plant' or 'vine'. The translation of the Jewish Publication Society of America is 'of the stock which thy right hand hath planted.' I have reversed the order of this and the following line.

page 96 *The Servant of God* S. I, 519; B. 154.
the way you pursue. i.e. the way in which God conducts himself, as it were, towards man; a way which man should imitate.
It is sin that makes a division . . . Cf. Isaiah 59, 2: 'But your iniquities have separated Between you and your God, And your sins have hid His face from you.'
Employ me. The use of the Hebrew verb, *qanah*, implies 'purchase' as well as 'creation'. The implications are manifold, including the idea that the poet wishes once more to be proclaimed God's servant, like the Israelites at the time of the Exodus, who were redeemed from Egyptian bondage in order to be created the servants of God.
'Here am I'. The Biblical phrase used by one replying to a divine summons. The poet's image of God using this phrase is both daring, and pregnant with meaning concerning the dialogue between man and God.

page 98 *Heal me, my God* S. I, 527.
The Arabic inscription at the head of this poem reads: 'Said when he was about to drink a healing medicine.' (Schirmann). Halevi practised medicine.
Heal me, my God, and I shall be healed. A quotation from Jeremiah 17, 14, included, with a change from singular to plural, in the *Amidah* prayer (Singer, 49).

page 99 *Singing God's Praise* S. I, 527.
On the interconnection between the praise offered by the angels and that offered by man, see the notes on 'Sanctification', page 149.
All the stars of the morning sing to you. Cf. Job 38, 7: '. . . the morning stars sang together, And all the sons of God shouted for joy.'

page 100 *My Heart is in the East* S. I, 489; B. 179.
Here begins a series of poems based on the poet's yearning to visit the Holy Land. See the Biographical Introduction.

my pledges and my vows. i.e. the poet's vows to travel to the Holy Land.

in the power of Edom. i.e. in Christian hands, since the conquest of Palestine by the Crusaders in 1099.

in the fetters of Arabia. i.e. in Muslim territory, Spain.

page 101 *Jerusalem* S. I, 489; B. 183.

Beautiful heights. Cf. Psalm 48, 3; 'Fair in situation, the joy of the whole earth; Even mount Zion, the uttermost parts of the north, The city of the great King.'

Your glory in exile. i.e. the Divine Presence which, according to a Rabbinic tradition, followed the Jews into exile.

Gilead's balm. Cf. Jeremiah 8, 22; 46, 11.

page 102 *Mount Avarim* S. I, 490.

Mount Avarim. Or Mount Nebo (Deut. 32, 49) where Moses died.

On you was gathered the best of men. Cf. Deut. 32, 50: 'die in the mount whither thou goest up, and be gathered unto thy people'

he was not a man of words Cf. Exodus 4, 10: 'And Moses said unto the Lord: "Oh Lord, I am not a man of words ... for I am slow of speech, and of a slow tongue." '

page 103 *Self-exhortation to Make the Journey to Israel* S. I, 494; B. 180.

The One whom all that will may seek. Brody's text reads 'The One who may be sought for anything.'

for your journey. A double-entendre, referring both to the particular journey to the Holy Land, and to the journey towards the life to come.

for a lentil-stew. A reference to Esau's sale of his birthright to Jacob (Genesis 25, 29ff.). Here, it is an image of material pleasure.

Your desire continually conceives new pleasures. lit. 'your desire produces new fruit every month'. I have reversed the order of this and the succeeding verse.

Do not confront him with magic and sorcery. The reference here is to Balaam (Numbers 24, 1ff.), the pagan seer, who had not the power to resist God's demands.

Be strong like a leopard. Cf. 'Ethics of the Fathers' 5, 23: 'Judah, the son of Tema, said: Be strong as a leopard, light as an eagle, fleet as a hart, and strong as a lion, to do the will of thy Father who is in heaven.' (Singer 274f.)

Let your heart remain firm ... Cf. Psalm 46, 3: 'Therefore will we not

165

fear, though the earth do change, And though the mountains be moved into the heart of the seas.'

The fir-trees. i.e. the ship's planks and beams made of the fir-tree.

Sand thrown into the sea. i.e. the ship's ballast, quantities of which were thrown overboard as necessity dictated (Schirmann).

'*Foul hearts are pure now.*' A confession of sin, and a prayer for forgiveness and rescue.

The merits of your holy forbears. The merits of the patriarchs which are considered to be efficacious for their descendants.

Mahlim and Mushim. Levitical families (Num. 3, 33) whose descendants would have sung and danced in the Temple. They are referred to here, since they are regarded by the poet, a Levite, as his own ancestors.

when the sun enters the ascent of the stars. lit. 'when the sun sinks through the degrees of the heavenly host.' The description is that of the rise of the moon and the stars as the sun sets.

the moon, their captain. lit. 'captain of fifty'. Cf. Isaiah 3, 3. There is possibly an allusion here to the poet's age.

bewildered in the heart of the sea. This and the following verses describe the reflection of the sky in the sea at night, and their apparent intermingling at the horizon.

page 106 *The Poet is Urged to Remain in Spain* S. I, 497; B. 187.

the most precious mountain. Mount Zion.

Philistines, Hittites, and descendants of Hagar. The Berbers are designated as Philistines, aud the Arabs as the descendants of Hagar. See Notes on pages 154 and 162. Who the Hittites are meant to represent is not clear.

Kiryath-yearim. The place where the ark remained for twenty years after its return from the Philistines (I Sam. 6, 21-7, 2).

for the ark and tablets buried there. The ark contained the tablets. See Yoma 52b: 'When the ark was hidden, there was hidden with it the bottles containing the manna, and that containing the sprinkling water . . . and the chest which the Philistines had sent as a gift to the God of Israel . . . Who hid it?—Josiah hid it.' See also 53a—54b.

where the cherubim and the engraved stones . . . I have transposed this and the following verse to this point in the poem, in accordance with a note by Schirmann. The cherubim were placed on each side of the ark in the Holy of Holies in the Temple (See Exodus 25, 18ff.). 'The engraved stones' refers to the two tablets of the Ten Commandments.

Mount Avarim. Where Moses died. See the poem 'Mount Avarim'.

the raising of the dead. A rabbinic tradition holds that at the coming of the Messiah, the Jews will be resurrected in the Holy Land.

the home of miracles, the fount of prophecy. According to Ha-Levi's philosophy, as expressed in 'The Kuzari' (see especially II, 14), all prophecy was spoken in the Holy Land or about the Holy Land.

the Shechinah's abode. Shechinah means the Divine Presence which has its home particularly in the Holy Land.

through the narrow passes. This refers to the difficult path of atonement and salvation. The Hebrew term is used in Psalm 116, 3 ('the straits of Sheol'), and the phrase used here is from Lamentations 1, 3: 'All her pursuers overtook her within the straits.'

page 109 *The Poet Remembers his Home* S. I, 501; B. 183.

the garden I have planted. This refers apparently to the circle of disciples which the poet formed in Spain (Schirmann).

Produce of my sun, the finest crop of my moon. Cf. Deuteronomy 33, 14: '. . . for the precious things of the fruits of the sun, And for the precious things of the yield of the moons.'

on my hands and knees. lit. 'on my hand and face', an image of his subservience to other men.

the footstool. i.e. the sanctuary in Jerusalem.

the gates of the skies. Cf. Genesis 28, 17: 'this is none other than the house of God, and this is the gate of heaven.'

Shiloach. A fountain and pool, south-east of Jerusalem.

page 111 *The Poet Remembers his Family during a Storm at Sea* S. I, 502.

Learning from my inmost fears. i.e. the sea is troubled as the poet himself is troubled.

As the ships of the Kittim come to the Philistine sea. The Kittim represent the Romans in Rabbinic sources. Here the Christians are meant. The Philistine sea would be the Western Mediterranean which washes the coast of the Berber territories. See note on page 154.

the Hittites. The reference is not clear. They may, according to Schirmann, denote North African pirates.

Your pleasant name will be continually in my mouth. lit. 'I shall place your pleasant name in my mouth for food.'

my heart. lit. my liver.

How can Judah ever forget Judah? i.e. How can the grandfather, Judah, ever forget his grandson, Judah?

your love. i.e. the love for God.

page 113 *The Western Breeze* S. I, 504.

the store-house of the wind. Cf. Psalm 135, 7: 'He bringeth forth the wind out of his treasuries.'

chained to his Rock. i.e. solely dependent upon God. lit. 'bound by the hand of the Rock.'

At one time confined, at another set free. Schirmann interprets this as referring to the journey of a ship, sometimes becalmed, sometimes swiftly moving. It may also refer generally to the life of the Jew.

page 114 *Storm at Sea* I and II S. I, 505.

Until I dance in your midst. The Hebrew has the specific meaning of 'to celebrate a festival'.

page 115 *The Army of Old Age* S. I, 444.

page 116 *To Moses ibn Ezra in Christian Spain* S. I, 461.

For the background to this poem see the biographical introduction to Moses ibn Ezra on page 75. According to the inscription to this poem, Moses ibn Ezra was living in Estella, in Navarre.

your departure would have made my death complete. The poet says that Moses' departure almost deprives him of life. Only the hope of his return keeps Judah alive.

mountains of Bether. Cf. Cant. 2, 17 (where the Jewish version translates 'mountains of spices'). The Hebrew word *Bether* comes from a root meaning 'to cut' or 'to divide'. We might, therefore, translate 'mountains of separation'.

Return to the West. The term 'West' was used generally by poets of the period to indicate Muslim Spain.

lamp of the West. In addition to the obvious metaphorical meaning of this phrase, Schirmann notes its association with the passage in *Menahot* 86b which describes how the western lamp of the Temple candelabrum, although containing no more oil than the others miraculously burned longer.

Gilboa. A mountain cursed by David in 2 Sam. 1, 21: 'Ye mountains of Gilboa, Let there be no dew nor rain upon you.'

page 117 *Among the Jews of Seville* S. I, 447.

the Tree of Life . . . the Tree of Knowledge. i.e. the Jews of Seville think that material prosperity will bring them eternal life, and so they despise the search for wisdom.

The herd of beasts crouch continually by the wall. A picture of the Seville Jews at prayer. Cf. Isaiah 38, 2: 'Then Hezekiah turned his face to the wall, and prayed unto the Lord.'

braggart but corrupt. lit. 'who have raised their horn on high, but it is cut down.'

Meir. Abulhassan Meir ibn Kamniah, of a noble Seville family. He held high office in Spain, and later was physician to the Almoravide rulers in Fez (Schirmann). A patron of poets, he was celebrated also in the verses of Moses ibn Ezra.

Just as Aaron was worthy. I have reversed the order of this and the following line.

page 119 *The Apple* S. I, 440.

page 120 *My Love Washes her Clothes* S. I, 439.

ABRAHAM IBN EZRA

page 123 *Luckless I* S. I, 575; B. 208.

Abraham ibn Ezra was a fervent believer in astrology. Here he maintains that the spheres altered their natural positions when he was born.

page 123 *Luckless II* S. I, 576; B. 209.

page 124 *I Have a Garment* S. I, 576.

The author of this poem is unknown, but, because of its subject-matter, it has been attributed to Abraham ibn Ezra.

would be superfluous. There is not enough of the garment remaining for a repair to be made.

page 125 *God Supreme* S. I, 600.

Praised be his glory. This refers to the prayer with which this poem was meant to be associated. The leader of the service calls: 'Praise ye the Lord who is to be praised' and the congregation respond: 'Praised is the Lord who is to be praised for ever and ever.' (Singer 38).

Through the prophets' inner sight. lit. 'and through the words of the prophets.'

page 126 *All Glory to his Name* S. I, 608.

All glory to his name. A reference to the first line of the *Kaddish* the prayer with which this poem is meant to be associated. The first line of the *Kaddish* (Singer 78) reads: 'Magnified and sanctified be his great name.'

who has numbered the world. i.e. God has complete knowledge of the world since he it was who created it.

his servants of fire. lit. those who minister to him, i.e. the angelic hosts, often described as beings of fire.

on the waters above. i.e. the waters above the firmament.

He moved his lips. The heavens were clothed. A quotation from Job 26, 13: 'By His breath the heavens are clear.' In his comment on this verse, Ibn Ezra himself implies that the Hebrew may refer to God's stretching out the heavens like a tent.

page 127 *How is it you have not Given this Thought?* S. I, 596; B. 203.

your battle-friends. i.e. those elements in the human personality which serve to combat the sensual impulses.

Put your wine back into the vault. lit. 'remove your wine'.

Once for your Creator, many times for you alone. You repent once before God, but satisfy your own evil desires many times.

before your Lord's court. i.e. on the day of judgment.

All the links that we have wrought. i.e. the links wrought between the soul and the body.

page 129 *On the Death of his Son, Isaac* S. I, 580; B. 205.

This is one of two laments that the poet composed on the death of his son, Isaac. Isaac left Spain in the same year as his father, but travelled to Egypt, and later to Baghdad. He became a convert to Islam, perhaps as a result of persecution, for he tells us in a poem on the subject (S. I, 628) 'I speak with my mouth—but my heart tells me: "You are a deceiver and your testimony is invalid" ', implying that his conversion was superficial only. The year of Isaac's death is not known. The closing line of each stanza is a quotation from the Bible viz. Genesis 22, 2; 35, 29; 25, 19; 27, 30; 24, 14.

Your son, your only son . . . Cf. Genesis 22, 2: 'Take now thy son, thine only son, whom thou lovest, even Isaac.' The relevance of the Biblical story of Abraham and Isaac to the poet's own experience is obvious.

generations. Heb. *toledoth* which came to signify 'history'.

enter into his divided soul. lit. 'pass through his pieces', a reference to the covenant that God made with Abraham 'between the pieces' in Genesis, 15.

170

page 133 *The Doctor*. From *Sefer Sha'ashu'im* ed. I. Davidson, Berlin 1925 page 123.

The poem may not be original, and a slightly different version is found in *Ha-Mebakkesh* of Shem Tob ben Palquera.

angel of death. lit. 'angels of death'.

JUDAH AL-HARIZI

page 137 *A Secret Kept* S. II, 203; B. 252.

Abigail. See I Sam. 25, 3.

Esther. lit. 'the daughter of Abihail'. See Esther 2, 15.

page 138 *The Lute Sounds* B. 251.

SHEM TOV BEN JOSEPH PALQUERA

page 141 *If Fear is like a Rock* B. 288.

TODROS BEN JUDAH ABULAFIA

page 145 *From Prison I* S. II, 445.

For the circumstances of his imprisonment, see the Biographical Introduction.

From Prison II S. II, 445.

For all my limbs are shaking with fear. lit. 'for my legs and my ankles tremble.'

my swallows. i.e. my children.

Index of First Lines

Index of First Hebrew Words

175

Printed and bound by CPI Group (UK) Ltd, Croydon, CR0 4YY

13/04/2025

14656583-0002